Health Promotion and Public Health

for Nursing Students

Transforming Nursing Practice series

Transforming Nursing Practice is the first series of books designed to help students meet the requirements of the NMC Standards and Essential Skills Clusters for degree programmes. Each book addresses a core topic, and together they cover the generic knowledge required for all fields of practice. Accessible and challenging, Transforming Nursing Practice helps nursing students prepare for the demands of future healthcare delivery.

Core knowledge titles:

Series editor: Dr Shirley Bach, Head of the School of Nursing and Midwifery at the University of Brighton

Communication and Interpersonal Skills in Nursing (2nd edn)	ISBN 978 0 85725 449 8
Contexts of Contemporary Nursing (2nd edn)	ISBN 978 1 84445 374 0
Health Promotion and Public Health for Nursing Students	ISBN 978 0 85725 437 5
Introduction to Medicines Management in Nursing	ISBN 978 1 84445 845 5
Law and Professional Issues in Nursing (2nd edn)	ISBN 978 1 84445 372 6
Leadership, Management and Team Working in Nursing	ISBN 978 0 85725 453 5
Learning Skills for Nursing Students	ISBN 978 1 84445 376 4
Medicines Management in Adult Nursing	ISBN 978 1 84445 842 4
Medicines Management in Children's Nursing	ISBN 978 1 84445 470 9
Medicines Management in Mental Health Nursing	ISBN 978 0 85725 049 0
Nursing Adults with Long Term Conditions	ISBN 978 0 85725 441 2
Nursing and Collaborative Practice (2nd edn)	ISBN 978 1 84445 373 3
Nursing and Mental Health Care	ISBN 978 1 84445 467 9
Passing Calculations Tests for Nursing Students	ISBN 978 1 84445 471 6
Patient and Carer Participation in Nursing	ISBN 978 0 85725 307 1
Successful Practice Learning for Nursing Students (2nd edn)	ISBN 978 0 85725 315 6
What is Nursing? Exploring Theory and Practice (2nd edn)	ISBN 978 0 85725 445 0

Personal and professional learning skills titles:

Joint series editors: Dr Mooi Standing, Principal Lecturer/Enterprise Quality Manager in the Department of Nursing and Applied Clinical Studies, Canterbury Christ Church University and Dr Shirley Bach, Head of the School of Nursing and Midwifery at the University of Brighton

Clinical Judgement and Decision Making in Nursing	ISBN 978 1 84445 468 6
Critical Thinking and Writing for Nursing Students	ISBN 978 1 84445 366 5
Evidence-based Practice in Nursing	ISBN 978 1 84445 369 6
Information Skills for Nursing Students	ISBN 978 1 84445 381 8
Reflective Practice in Nursing	ISBN 978 1 84445 371 9
Succeeding in Research Project Plans and Literature Reviews for Nursing Students	ISBN 978 0 85725 264 7
Successful Professional Portfolios for Nursing Students	ISBN 978 0 85725 457 3
Understanding Research for Nursing Students	ISBN 978 1 84445 368 9

To order, contact our distributor: BEBC Distribution, Albion Close, Parkstone, Poole, BH12 3LL. Telephone: 0845 230 9000, email: learningmatters@bebc.co.uk. You can also find more information on each of these titles and our other learning resources at **www.learningmatters.co.uk**. Many of these titles are also available in various e-book formats, please visit our website for more information.

Health Promotion and Public Health

for Nursing Students

Daryl Evans
Dina Coutsaftiki
C. Patricia Fathers

Learning Matters

First published in 2011 by Learning Matters Ltd

©2011 Daryl Evans, Dina Coutsaftiki and C. Patricia Fathers

British Library Cataloguing in Publication Data
A CIP record for this book is available from the British Library

ISBN: 978 0 85725 437 5

This book is also available in the following ebook formats:

Adobe ebook ISBN:	978 0 85725 439 9
ePub ebook ISBN:	978 0 85725 438 2
Kindle ISBN:	978 0 85725 440 5

25666452

The rights of Daryl Evans, Dina Coutsaftiki and C. Patricia Fathers to be identified as the authors of this Work has been asserted by them in accordance with the Copyright, Designs and Patents Act 1988.

Cover and text design by Toucan Design
Project management and typesetting by 4word Ltd, Page & Print Production
Printed and bound in Great Britain by Short Run Press, Exeter, Devon

Learning Matters Ltd
20 Cathedral Yard
Exeter EX1 1HB
Tel: 01392 215560
E-mail: info@learningmatters.co.uk
www.learningmatters.co.uk

FSC
www.fsc.org
MIX
Paper from
responsible sources
FSC® C014540

Contents

Foreword

It is easy to imagine that nurses are only involved in supporting the sick to recover and the long-term ill to have an optimum quality of life. Yet nurses have an equally important role in promoting the health and well-being of patients. Thinking about where to begin with this aspect of the role is often a challenge, as the more obvious role model is a nurse who makes people feel better after they have become ill. The authors of this text have taken a very different approach to stimulating this by encouraging readers to think in a health-promoting way right from the start. The first chapter tackles this idea head-on and gives readers a fundamental introduction to what it means to be healthy and the different interpretations of that concept.

The text continues to explore and explain, in very accessible language, how a nurse can develop techniques to support and promote the health, well-being, rights and dignity of individual people, groups, communities and populations identified in the NMC standards. Techniques to conduct sensitive conversations about tackling lifestyle change are covered, as well as methods to keep the reader informed about the ever-developing research on health advice. There is a well-balanced chapter on screening which is both informative and evaluative of the services available.

The next section of the text explores the role of the individual in determining his or her own health choices. This is examined from the health education perspective with practical ideas and techniques to integrate into daily practice. The next chapter concentrates on the concept of self management and what that really means in contemporary health care.

The following chapters broaden the reader's perspective to look at the role of health promotion in public health and the role of the nurse in addressing the social determinants of health and unhealthy environments. This might seem a big step to take, but nurses do have a part to play and the text examines the steps nurses can take in planning services and projects that can have a positive impact on the health of communities. The final chapter provides the readers with practical tips on how to keep up with current practice and gives some ideas on the compilation of the portfolio which is required to meet professional standards in health promotion. You can be assured that you will be a health promotion thinker by the end of the text and your knowledge and understanding of a topic that is often hard to grasp will be much more sound.

Shirley Bach
Series Editor

About the authors

Daryl Evans is a principal lecturer in nursing and health promotion at Middlesex University, where she is programme leader for the BSc Health Promotion (top-up) course. She is an experienced nurse and nurse teacher and integrates health promotion practice into her role at the university. Her professional interests include empowerment of patients, settings-based health promotion and teaching analysis skills to nurses.

Dina Coutsaftiki is a senior lecturer in nursing and health promotion at Middlesex University, where she teaches on pre-registration and post-registration courses. She also acts as a supervisor for students' dissertations at first degree and master's level. She has been in academia since 1989 and has a diverse clinical background in nursing, ranging across acute general medicine, surgery and gynaecology. She is a clinical specialist in reproductive and sexual health. Her research interests are in health promotion with special focus on reproductive health.

C. Patricia Fathers is a senior lecturer at Middlesex University and teaches on the BSc Health Promotion (top-up) course. She has taught health promotion to both nursing students and multidisciplinary healthcare students. This role has provided some insight into the needs of students as they engage in the study of health promotion.

Introduction

Who is this book for?

This book is written for students of nursing who are developing knowledge and skills in health promotion and public health. Although primarily aimed at students, it will also be useful for qualified nurses improving their practice and their role as mentors to students. Any health professional undertaking health promotion in their practice may find aspects of the book helpful for reviewing what they do and planning improvements.

Health promotion and public health are essential components of the nurse's role. The knowledge and skills required may seem to be a vast volume of learning of a whole different subject in its own right. We intend this book to more directly apply what is relevant to nursing, and in particular to help the nursing student to understand how the topic specifically relates to them. The book will show how health promotion and public health is integral to any nurse's role, whether that be in primary (community), secondary (hospital) or tertiary (charity, independent and private) healthcare settings.

Book structure

We have decided to take a less conventional approach than usual in selecting the topics in each chapter. Our experience in practising health promotion and public health within nursing has taught us that theories and principles need to be applied to the real world of nursing.

We start the book with a chapter on 'Thinking health promotion'. We decided that nurses need to think about the subject of health promotion first, before considering the whole of public health. To think in the manner of a health promoter puts you into a set of ideas which are different to nursing and yet transferable into your practice. Instead of just defining health promotion, the chapter encourages you to see the international context and political dimensions of improving health. The chapter looks at theories informing health promotion and introduces two models of health promotion which are followed up in further chapters.

In Chapter 2, 'Tackling lifestyle change', we address directly one of the biggest issues, that of persuading and enabling people to live healthily through lifestyle choices. This enormous and often difficult-to-achieve goal is relevant to your work with individual patients and their families, and to your work with larger communities. Mostly nurses think that this is merely a case of giving more information, but the chapter illustrates that this may not be the answer. This chapter enables you to structure the way you give the best information and advice about making healthy lifestyle choices.

In Chapter 3 we have focused on encouraging health screening, as we feel that it is not given sufficient emphasis in nursing. Many screening systems exist in the NHS but nurses often know little about them. It is clear to us that being able to talk to patients about the pros and cons of screening is essential, even if you are not working in a screening system yourself. You can be the resource the patient or family member uses to find out what happens and whether they should attend.

Chapter 4 is about teaching patients. As it is fundamental to the nurse's role, the education of patients and their families is perhaps quite well understood by nurses. We contend, however, that its practice needs to be improved. Too often the teaching which a patient needs ends up as information-giving at the point of discharge from hospital, or not done becausenurses feel that there is not enough time to do it. The chapter gives some practical ideas and encouragement to make teaching patients a more integrated part of your daily practice.

Chapter 5, 'Supporting self-management', is a topic of increasing emphasis in the international literature. Health services must allocate more resources to enable the increasing number of people living with long-term conditions to help themselves. In the interests of cost-effective health care and in the interests of empowerment of patients, nurses must develop the skills to support self-management. The chapter includes some ideas and systems many nurses are as yet unaware of. Focusing on the learned tendency to provide care has made nurses less able to facilitate patients to become partners in their care.

The subject of Chapter 6, 'Considering public health', has been purposefully left until later in the book. Health promotion (as part of public health) is what nurses mostly do, but it is important to develop an awareness of the wider role. Even the public is developing a greater awareness of what public health can achieve, through news items about outbreaks of communicable disease and political debates about dealing with 'the obesity epidemic'. The chapter give you some ideas of the functions of public health and of your role in addressing the wider determinants of health and consequences of unhealthy environments.

Chapter 7, 'Managing health promotion in practice', helps you to develop a more coordinating and managing role in improving health. It looks at the idea of people being in settings where they work, live, learn and receive care. You will look at the professional skills you will continue to develop for public health and health promotion, skills related to project planning and partnership working.

Chapter 8, 'Keeping up your skills', is a chapter which challenges you to plan to learn more and gain more skills. The chapter includes useful and practical ways to keep up to date with information and to plan your lifelong learning. This chapter puts reflection, planning your learning and portfolio compilation into the context of health promotion.

Requirements for the NMC Standards for Pre-Registration Nursing Education and the Essential Skills Clusters

The Nursing and Midwifery Council (NMC) has established standards of competence to be met by applicants to different parts of the register, and these are the standards it considers necessary for safe and effective practice in relation to health promotion and public health. In addition to the competencies, the NMC has set out specific skills that nursing students must be able to perform at various points of an education programme. These are known as essential skills clusters (ESCs). This book is structured so that it will help you to understand and meet the competencies and ESCs required for entry to the NMC register. The relevant competencies and ESCs are presented at the start of each chapter so that you can clearly see which ones the chapter addresses. There are generic standards that all nursing students irrespective of their field must achieve, and field-specific standards relating to each field of nursing; i.e. mental health, children's, learning disability and adult nursing. This book includes the latest standards for 2010 onwards, taken from the *Standards for pre-registration nursing education* (NMC, 2010).

Learning features

Learning from reading text is not always easy. Therefore, to provide variety and to assist with the development of independent learning skills and the application of theory to practice, this book contains activities, case studies, scenarios, further reading, useful websites and other materials to enable you to participate in your own learning. You will need to develop your own study skills and 'learn how to learn' to get the best from the material. The book cannot provide all the answers, but instead provides a framework for your learning.

The activities in the book will in particular help you to make sense of, and learn about, the material being presented. Some activities ask you to reflect on aspects of practice, or your experience of it, or the people or situations you encounter. Reflection is an essential skill in nursing, and it helps you to understand the world around you and often to identify how things might be improved. Other activities will help you develop key graduate skills such as your ability to think critically about a topic in order to challenge received wisdom, or your ability to research a topic and find appropriate information and evidence, and to be able to make decisions using that evidence in situations that are often difficult and time-pressured. Communication and working as part of a team are core to all nursing practice, and some activities will ask you to carry out team work activities or think about your communication skills to help develop these.

All the activities require you to take a break from reading the text, think through the issues presented and carry out some independent study, possibly using the internet. Where appropriate, there are sample answers presented at the end of each chapter, and these will help you to understand more fully your own reflections and independent study. Remember, academic study will always require independent work; attending lectures will never be enough to be successful on your programme, and these activities will help to deepen your knowledge and understanding of the issues under scrutiny and give you practice at working on your own.

You might want to think about completing these activities as part of your personal development plan (PDP) or portfolio. After completing the activity write it up in your PDP or portfolio in a section devoted to that particular skill, then look back over time to see how far you are developing. You can also do more of the activities for a key skill that you have identified a weakness in, which will help build your skill and confidence in this area.

There is a glossary of terms at the end of the book which provides an interpretation of some key terminology in the context of the subject of the book. Glossary terms are in **bold** in the first instance that they appear.

All chapters have further reading and useful websites listed at the end, with notes to show you why we think they will be helpful to you.

We hope you enjoy this book and good luck with your studies!

Chapter 1
Thinking health promotion

NMC Standards for Pre-registration Nursing Education

This chapter will address the following competencies:

Domain 1: Professional values

2. All nurses must practise in a holistic, non-judgemental, caring and sensitive manner that avoids assumptions, supports social inclusion, recognises and respects individual choice and acknowledges diversity. Where necessary, they must challenge inequality, discrimination and exclusion from access to care.

3. All nurses must support and promote the health, wellbeing, rights and dignity of people, groups, communities and populations. These include people whose lives are affected by ill health, disability, ageing, death and dying. Nurses must understand how theses activities influence public health.

7. All nurses must appreciate the value of evidence in practice, be able to understand and appraise research, apply relevant theory and research findings to their work, and identify areas for further investigation.

Domain 3: Nursing practice and decision-making

5. All nurses must understand public health principles, priorities and practice in order to recognise and respond to the major causes and social determinants of health, illness and health inequalities. They must use a range of information and data to assess the needs of people, groups, communities and populations and work to improve health, wellbeing and experiences of healthcare; secure equal access to health screening, health promotion and healthcare and promote social inclusion.

NMC Essential Skills Clusters

This chapter will address the following ESC:

Cluster: Organisational aspects of care

9. People can trust the newly registered graduate nurse to treat them as partners and work with them to make a holistic and systematic assessment of their needs; to develop a personalised plan that is based on mutual understanding and respect for their individual situation promoting health and well-being, minimising risk of harm and promoting their safety at all times.

By the second progression point:

3. Understands the concept of public health and the benefits of healthy lifestyles and the potential risks involved with various lifestyles or behaviours, for example, substance misuse, smoking, obesity.

continued overleaf...

• • *continued...* •

By the third progression point:

4. Recognises indicators of unhealthy lifestyles.

18. Discusses sensitive issues in relation to public health and provides appropriate advice and guidance to individuals, communities and populations for example, contraception, substance misuse, smoking, obesity.

Chapter aims

By the end of this chapter you will be able to:

- define health and health promotion;
- discuss the contribution of the World Health Organization (WHO) to the development and practice of health promotion;
- appreciate the contribution of health promotion strategies to the promotion of good health and wellbeing;
- understand and integrate theories and models of health promotion to nursing practice.

Introduction

This chapter will encourage you to think health promotion. Thinking like a health-promoting nurse will enable you to integrate the principles and practice of health promotion into your nursing care. How do you think like a health promoter? Always have in mind that nurses can contribute to improving health in the broader sense while performing caring related to recovery from illness.

The chapter explores the concept of heath and how this informs your health promotion practice. It enables you to develop your knowledge and understanding of the health promotion concept and its contribution to improving the health and quality of life of the individual and the population at large. The chapter explores the origin of health promotion and discusses international and national health strategies and their contribution to the development of your health promotion practice. Theories and models of health are examined in order to enable you to structure your health promotion practice.

What does it mean to be healthy?

Case study: What does it mean to be healthy?

Abdul, a 52-year-old school teacher, underwent pancreatectomy and chemotherapy following a diagnosis of an advanced pancreatic cancer. As a result of removing his pancreas he is on insulin injections. He says:

I have accepted my diagnosis and now I want to live a normal life. I am confident and competent in self-injecting the prescribed insulin. Shahita, my partner, is my rock. We are able to set realistic and achievable daily goals. Since my illness we have adopted a healthy lifestyle. Our diet, including

continued opposite...

continued...

the diet of Leon (our dog), is much healthier and also we are more physically active. I take Leon for a walk in the nearby park daily. I enjoy the fresh air and meeting the regular dog walkers.

I am back to full time work. I enjoy teaching and I get a lot of personal satisfaction knowing that I contribute to my pupils' learning and development. I value the daily structure and social interaction offered by my work. I receive encouragement and support from my colleagues. We are able to have a laugh. However, I am aware that some colleagues feel that I am too ill to be working. They all know that my expected survival time is 18 months.

I have accepted that I do not have long to live, however 18 months is still a long time. I still have inspirations and dreams. I want the remainder of my life to be lived in full. Shahita and I decided to get married and to have a huge wedding in three months' time. I feel that I am doing the things I always wanted to do but somehow I never got around to doing them. I have made a will: I want to put my financial and private affairs into order before the inevitable happens.

Shahita and I talk a lot about death. I am not afraid of dying but I am afraid of how I will die. Will I be in pain? I am very lucky to live next door to Helen, a retired midwife and health visitor. I have known her all my life. She actually delivered me! I have frequent conversations with Helen, updating her with my medical progress, and I am able to seek her advice. She is able to explain things to me. I find her a great emotional support. I have very open and confidential conversations with Helen. I can shed a tear in front of Helen without feeling embarrassed or less of a man.

In the evenings I feel quite tired. I tend to spend most evenings reading the Qur'an or watching television. Some evenings my siblings will come to visit. I enjoy reminiscing with them about the past and the good old days. Overall I have good and bad days like everybody else.

The case study illustrates that different people have different views of what it means to be healthy. For example, some of Abdul's working colleagues view health as being free from disease. Abdul, on the other hand, is in remission and views health as personal fulfilment.

Exploring the concept of health

You need to develop a comprehensive understanding of the health concept because it informs and shapes your health promotion practice. One important point to bear in mind is that an individual's health status is not static. It is constantly changing throughout the day and is evolving throughout a lifetime. Have you noticed how you feel different at different times of the day, for example in the morning you may have felt very energetic and by midday you may feel exhausted, or how your mood fluctuates during the day?

Health encompasses the following different dimensions.

- Physical: this is quite obvious as it relates to the functions of your body, e.g. I am not well because I have a headache.
- Emotional: this can relate to how you cope with feelings such as anxiety, depression or your ability to recognise your own emotions such as fear and joy.
- Intellectual: this means that you have the ability to think clearly and coherently.

- Sexual: this means that you have the ability and freedom to establish intimate, loving relationships as well as choice and ability of procreation.
- Social: this means that you have the ability to make and maintain relationships with other people, e.g. having friends.
- Spiritual: this means that you are able to achieve peace of mind or are able to be in peace with your own self. As a nurse you must recognise this is not only associated with religion. People who do not have a religion can achieve spiritual health by adopting principles of behaviour which lead to spirituality.

Activity 1.1 is designed to enable you to develop a clear understanding of the above health dimensions.

Activity 1.1   *Critical thinking*

Review Abdul's case study shown earlier and discuss either with your peers or with a member of your family the following questions regarding Abdul's health.

- Is he physically healthy?
- Is he emotionally healthy?
- Is he intellectually healthy?
- Is he sexually healthy?
- Is he socially healthy?
- Is he spiritually healthy?

Were there any differences of opinion? Were all of you able to support your argument?

An outline answer is provided at the end of the chapter.

Activity 1.1 has demonstrated to you that health is a very difficult concept to define. When you discussed Abdul's health dimensions, what personal factors influenced your own assessment?

The meaning of health can be influenced by a multitude of factors such as family and cultural background, religion, educational level, gender, ethnicity and **social class**. Outside influences include the effects of the media, social environment and government policies. In addition, the individual's personal life experience will influence their views of health.

These influences apply equally to **lay** people and health professionals. For example, if you reflect back at the onset of starting your nursing course up to the present time, you may realise that your past and current views about health are different. This can be attributed to the influence of your professional socialisation in the clinical practice and the nursing knowledge you have gained. As a result your health views have been reshaped as you have been exposed to a new professional culture and have developed new expertise.

Lay perceptions

As a nurse you are working in **partnership** with your patients and their families, aiming to establish an interactive therapeutic relationship which encourages patients and families to participate in their care and to take responsibility for their health. Therefore, you need to give 'voice' and 'choice' to your patients (Department of Health, 2006a). To facilitate this process you have to seek out their health views. Knowing their health views enables you to design and implement health promotion programmes relevant to patients and communities.

Lay people's perspectives of health have been researched extensively over the last 40 years. Some people may view health:

- *in terms of not being ill* – 'I am well today because I do not have a cold or a headache';
- *in the context of physical fitness* – taking regular exercises and being fit;
- *in terms of control and risk* – binge drinking is seen as a health risk while being able to drink 'normal' amounts of alcohol is seen as being in control and having the ability to manage health;
- *in terms of not having a health problem which interferes with daily life* – an elderly person may consider being healthy as being able to walk or cook or going out to visit friends;
- *in the context of social relationships* – having friends and family around for social support and interaction;
- *as a psychosocial wellbeing* – emotional wellbeing is being happy and having recreational activities such as going on holidays.

As you can see, lay people's concept of health is diverse, ranging from the functional and medical perspective to psychosocial perspective. The different views are associated with social class issues, for example working class people may see health from the functional perspective while the higher **socio-economic** groups may see health from the psychosocial perspective. Age and gender are contributing factors; young men may view health from the physical activity perspective, while women may emphasise the social perspective of having friends and family around them. You need to address these influences when you plan your health promotion practice (Chapters 4 and 7), aiming to deliver a personalised health promotion practice which empowers your patient to improve their health status.

How do health professionals view the concept of health? Are there any differences between lay and professional views?

Professional concepts of health

Health professionals view the concept in relation to the following health models. Understanding the different models of health will enable you to understand how the different health professionals with whom you work interpret health and working in partnership (see Chapter 7) to develop a health promotion practice with common goals and objectives to improve your patients' health.

Medical model

Under the medical model of health your practice has a disease orientation instead of a positive health orientation. You view your patients only in terms of their presenting illnesses, therefore you focus on the physical dimension of health without taking into consideration the other dimensions of health previously discussed in this chapter. This means that you view each patient as a body (which includes brain function) in terms of possible defective parts and your aim is to repair the part. It means that you medically manage the diagnosis and your health promotion focuses on teaching patients such things as how to use their inhalers to improve their breathing without considering other factors which may influence recovery such as personal circumstances and health inequalities.

In summary, from the health promotion and public health perspective (Chapter 6) the main focus in the medical model is on treatment and cure. However, a health promotion perspective can be achieved by viewing your patient as a whole.

Holistic model

A well-documented and widely used definition of health by many health professionals is that of the World Health Organization (WHO, 1948): *Health is a state of complete physical, mental and social wellbeing and not merely the absence of disease.* The combination of physical, social and mental wellbeing is known as the 'health triangle'.

The model expands on the medical model of health by embracing the concept of wellbeing. However, the definition implies a utopian view of achievement of health. It is therefore, arguably, idealistic in that it is impossible to attain a 'complete state' of health. One may also argue that it excludes people like Abdul (terminal illnesses) or people with chronic diseases (schizophrenia, Parkinson's), or disability (visual impairment or learning disabilities) or people who, due to circumstances beyond their control such as poverty, are unable to achieve optimum health.

In health promotion terms the **holistic** approach emphasises the need to integrate health education and prevention activities which are evidence-based practice. Your practice has to be informed not only by the medical aspects of health but also by local and national health strategies. The model encourages a re-orientation of NHS provision from the acute health **sector** to primary care (community health sector).

The wellness model

The WHO, moving with social trends and political ideologies, developed the concept of health further by developing a wellness model which is build on the principles of the holistic model.

The Ottawa Charter for health promotion considered health to be not just a 'state', but also is seen as a *resource for everyday life, not the objective of living. It is a positive concept emphasising social and personal resources, as well as physical capabilities* (WHO, 1986). This definition is relevant to current health promotion practice, which strives to improve quality of life of all people regardless of their health status. It includes healthy people, people with disabilities, people with mental health issues, people with learning disabilities and people with long-term conditions. It highlights the need for the individual to be resilient by adapting to life changes such as illnesses and changes in socio-economic circumstances.

The model encourages health professionals to promote antidiscriminatory practice. For example, you as a health promoter, through the application of an empowering approach to your practice (Chapter 5), will support people with physical impairment, such as wheelchair users, to secure employment and lead an independent life. You will act as an enabler to facilitate them to adapt positively to life's changes and to strive for personal growth and fulfilment by developing problem-solving skills and increasing their **self-esteem**.

Thinking about the complexities of health through the different perspectives of the three models discussed above could be confusing. We suggest that you consider the WHO 1948 definition of health in combination with their 1986 definition of health as a resource.

In this way nurses can act in partnership with other healthcare professionals, patients and their families, to devise an eclectic model of health incorporating the three components of body (physical), mind (mental) and community (social) aspects of health as well as the ability of people to gain control of their own health (adapting and growing).

To assist you we will be looking in future chapters at:

- enabling your patients to change their health behaviours (Chapter 2);
- empowering them to understand their illnesses (Chapter 4);
- supporting them to 'self-manage' their illnesses (Chapter 5).

However, before you develop your nursing practice to integrate health promotion principles, you need to have a deeper understanding of the health promotion concept.

Defining health promotion

Health promotion is about improving the health status of individuals and the population as a whole. Key to the term health promotion is the word promotion. This means placing the notion of the absence of disease and wellbeing at the forefront of your nursing practice. This shift in emphasis will help you think about improving, advancing, encouraging and supporting your patients to achieve optimum health. These activities are all part of a health-promoting perspective.

Today health promotion is an important focus of UK public policy in all sectors, with an emphasis on the social and environmental aspects as much as the physical and mental. Therefore, nurses have to view health promotion from both a holistic and a wellness model of health. It is helpful to understand the major socio-economic determinants of health. Very often these are outside the control of the individual but can have an enormous effect on the individual's health, for example, employment redundancy may lead to poverty and may affect the individual's physical health and mental health, such as increased smoking or depression.

The fundamental aim of health promotion is to empower an individual or a community to take control of aspects of their lives which have a detrimental effect on their health. The WHO (1986) defines health promotion as 'a process of enabling people to increase control over, and to improve, their health'. This definition implies that you need to act as an enabler by strengthening knowledge, attitudes, skills and capabilities of your patients to overcome negative health. Additionally governments are urged by the WHO to formulate health strategies to facilitate this enabling process.

Activity 1.2 aims to encourage you to explore the scope of health promotion. The activity gives a selection of activities which you may consider to be health promoting.

Which of the following activities do you consider to be health promoting by enabling or empowering?

- TV advertisement around the Christmas period which encourages the public 'not to drink and drive';
- radio message on your local radio encouraging young people to ring a helpline if they feel that they are victims of abuse;
- practice nurses delivering a smoking cessation programme;
- nurses teaching carers how to feed their loved one at home via a PEG (percutaneous endoscopic gastrostomy) feeding tube;
- legislation on compulsory use of car seat belts;
- Jamie Oliver **lobbying** the government for the implementation of healthy school meals;
- local authorities organising park walks for young mothers;
- health agencies such as Age UK giving information during winter on how to keep warm;
- environmental health officers inspecting restaurants and cafes to monitor hygiene standards;
- restaurants providing food information on their menu such as the fat content of their lamb moussaka;
- practice nurses immunising older people against the flu virus;
- nurses washing their hands;
- student nurses receiving moving and handling training;
- supporting people with learning disabilities to use public transport.

An outline answer is provided at the end of the chapter.

A very broad range of activities can be considered to be part of health promotion. If the broader views of health are accepted (holistic and wellness), then health promotion matches that breadth. Acting on socio-environmental, as well as physical, influences on health enables us to accept that many people, professionals, organisations and government work to promote health in all sorts of ways, as you can see in Activity 1.2 and in the next section. This modern view of the potential for improving health began in the 1980s with an international shift in emphasis to give this broader range.

The origin of health promotion

Health promotion gained momentum in the global **health agenda** in the latter part of the twentieth century. This took place against a backdrop of discontent and frustration in international political and public opinion with the status quo of the medically dominated healthcare systems. Those systems were failing to combat ill health and to meet the health needs of the populations they were serving, despite a constant increase in financial investment.

Health promotion emerged as a process to shift healthcare provision away from a hospital setting centred on the medicalisation of health towards a community setting informed by the principles of public health (Chapter 6). This transition was facilitated as the holistic and wellbeing models of health started to gain momentum and the dominant medical model started to be eroded.

The WHO has been instrumental in the development of health promotion. Its commitment to use health promotion to improve global health is seen in a number of international charters and declarations on health. The most significant are the Ottawa Charter, the Adelaide Conference and the Bangkok Charter.

Concept summary: The Ottawa Charter (WHO, 1986)

This charter created the following principles for health promotion action which are still relevant today.

Build healthy public policy

Health promotion goes beyond healthcare. **Policy** makers across all government sectors must consider health consequences and accept responsibility for health. This means when considering transport or housing or employment policies at local or national level they should be asking about their health implications. In addition policy decisions should be made to improve health from central government, such as the smoking ban.

Create supportive environments

The environment we live in affects our health, for example changing patterns of life, work and leisure and our natural environment have a significant impact on our health. Therefore health promotion has to influence the generation of living and working conditions that are safe, stimulating, satisfying and enjoyable (Chapter 7).

Strengthen community action

Health promotion works through concrete and effective community action in setting priorities, making decisions, planning and implementing them to achieve better health. At the heart of this process is community empowerment (Chapter 7).

Develop personal skills

Health promotion supports personal and social development through the provision of information, education or health enhancing **life skills**. Health promotion has to enable people to learn, throughout life, to prepare themselves for all its health-related problems and to cope with long-term conditions and injuries (Chapters 4 and 5).

Re-orient health services

The role of the health sector must move beyond its traditional responsibility for providing curative and clinical health. In the UK the NHS should focus more on prevention of illness and promotion of positive wellness.

The Ottawa Charter remains as one of the most influential charters within the field of health promotion and public health. It is based on a **strategy** of enabling people to control health, advocating that health must be prioritised in all sectors and mediating between possible partners to improve health.

Following on from Ottawa, The Adelaide Conference (WHO, 1988) brought health promotion practice to new levels with health being viewed as a 'human right'. Health was no longer to be seen as a mere commodity. The conference introduced the concept of **equity**, highlighting that all people and patients have to be treated the same.

Later, the Bangkok Charter (WHO, 2005) urged all global governments to integrate effective health promotion interventions into their domestic and foreign policies. They are asked to implement interventions which have been proven to contribute to positive health and wellbeing into everything they do, whether it is town planning, road expansion or financial cutbacks. Policies, not only in times of peace but also in times of war and conflict, need to be 'healthy', so, for example, nurses who are currently working in the armed forces in the war zone of Afghanistan have to use a repertoire of evidence-based health interventions to promote a sense of wellbeing to the soldiers.

The WHO, in addition to international charters and declarations, has placed health promotion at the heart of its current global health agenda by its health for all policy in the twenty-first century (World Health Assembly, 1998) by continuing the previous vision of the health for all by the year 2000 strategy (WHO, 1978).

Concept summary: WHO health for all (HFA) policy for the twenty-first century

The policy calls for social justice, which means that each person should be treated fairly and equitably. It lists ten global health targets set out in three domains, reflecting the most prevalent health problems in the world.

Improving health outcomes

- Health equity: this will be assessed by measuring a child's growth, i.e. height and weight levels for age (children under five years).
- Survival: to improve maternal mortality rates, child mortality rates (under five years) and life expectancy.
- Reverse global trends of five major pandemics (TB, malaria, HIV/AIDS, tobacco-related diseases and violence/trauma) by implementing disease control programmes.
- Eradicate and eliminate certain diseases (measles, leprosy, vitamin A and iodine deficiencies).

Determinants of health

- Improve access to water, sanitation, food and shelter.
- Measures to enhance healthy lifestyles and weaken damaging ones.

continued opposite...

continued...

Health policies

- Develop, implement and monitor national HFA policies.
- Improve access to comprehensive essential quality healthcare.
- Implement global and national health information and surveillance systems.
- Support research for health.

Each region of the WHO (Africa, Americas, South East Asia, Europe, Eastern Mediterranean, and Western Pacific) and subsequently individual countries have modified and incorporated this strategy into their own strategies to meet the health needs of the populations which they serve. The WHO (1998a) developed a strategy for Europe known as Health 21.

The following case study outlines the different global health challenges.

Case study: Different global health challenges

Mrs Shah, a registered nurse, has returned to England after spending two years working as a volunteer nurse in one of Africa's underdeveloped countries. She gives a seminar to her work colleagues, aiming to share her working experience in Africa.

Her account supports the need for a global health strategy and highlights the importance of gaining the political commitment of international organisations, as well as national government, to implement the WHO's strategy. In summary Nurse Shah highlighted:

Every day, people of all ages in sub-Saharan Africa die unnecessarily. The main cause is infectious diseases such as malaria, tuberculosis, HIV/AIDS and diarrhoea. One of the biggest challenges healthcare providers face is the delivery of adequate healthcare for people living with chronic lifestyle conditions. People in rural areas have to walk many miles to access care. Many die in transit.

Another frustrating thing for me was the fact that healthcare professionals work in isolation, particularly those working in rural settings, and could not keep abreast with the latest information on epidemics. This also precludes them from sharing their information with the global health community. Nurses in the region are increasingly faced with the burden of providing healthcare to rural populations, much more than the doctors. Enhancing health professionals', especially nurses' access to relevant accurate and up-to-date clinical information is vital to improving healthcare.

Recognising aspects of the international view of health promotion will help you to understand the global background to what is happening in the UK, strategically and politically. As a member state of WHO (European Region) the UK is instrumental in helping to formulate the international strategies, and in turn to an extent follows those strategies.

UK national strategic policies for public health and health promotion

In the UK the concept of health promotion can be dated as far back as the nineteenth century, forming part of the public health movement for sanitary reforms to improve the ill health of people living in overcrowded industrial towns. Florence Nightingale embraced the principles of public health to inform nursing practice (Nightingale, 1859).

The first ever public health strategy published in the UK was *The Health of the Nation* (Department of Health, 1992) by the then Conservative government. This was superseded by the strategies of the new Labour government *Saving lives: Our Healthier Nation* (Department of Health 1999) and later, *Choosing Health: Making Healthier Choices Easier* (Department of Health, 2004a). Scotland, Wales and Northern Ireland had their own similar strategies.

All these health strategies use health promotion to facilitate the achievement of **health improvement** and to encourage people to 'make healthy choices easier', a political jargon originated by the WHO and used to achieve **health gain**. The policies aim to improve health of the individual and the population by addressing the wider issues which affect health such as health inequalities and environmental issues.

The current UK coalition government has produced its own strategy, *Healthy Lives, Healthy People: Our Strategy for Public Health in England* (Department of Health, 2010a). It focuses on behaviour change strategies by encouraging individuals to engage in healthy behaviour and to take more control and responsibility for their own health, thereby moving away from the notion of the 'nanny state' whereby people expect the state to take care of their own health (Chapters 2 and 6).

As the various successive governments endeavour to improve people's health and to promote positive health, healthcare professionals have witnessed the establishment of the following:

- NHS Direct: this was launched in 1998 as a nurse-led telephone helpline and internet service providing information and advice on health to the public. The current coalition government is proposing to phase out the NHS Direct telephone number in favour of a new non-emergency number in order to make financial savings.
- NICE (National Institute for Health and Clinical excellence): responsible for providing national guidance on promoting good health, and preventing and treating ill health.
- Public Health Observatories: established in 2000 in each NHS region. Their role is to ensure that health and social care systems are equipped with health intelligence to improve health and reduce inequalities, to promote research and to set up disease registers.
- Health Protection Agency (HPA): set up in 2003 to protect the public from infectious diseases and environmental hazards. The HPA is one of a number of quangos (quasi-autonomous non-governmental organisations) which the current government will abolish. This protection function will be transferred to central NHS control.
- Patient Advice and Liaison services (PALS): designed to bring citizens more closely to decision-making processes.
- Expert patients programmes: to help people manage their own illnesses (see Chapter 5).

- NHS walk-in centres: managed by local community health organisations to deal with minor illnesses and injuries and are predominately nurse led.
- Polyclinics: established on the recommendations of Lord Darzi (a parliamentary under-secretary in the House of Lords), they are a network of GPs in multi-purpose health centres, who provide some hospital services, i.e. x-rays, minor surgery and out-patients treatment.

As well as these strategic innovations, we have seen a focus on addressing **inequalities in health** which has been informed by WHO's work (see Chapter 6 for a fuller explanation).

We now go on to look at health promotion theories and models to guide your work. We previously looked at theories of health; however, theory is also important to 'thinking health promotion' as without it we may act randomly and without the evidence to support practice. Theoretical structures are based on ideas from philosophical or organisational constructs and more recently deduced from practice itself. You will find health promotion theories used throughout this book; here we give an overview of the most important ones. A model, as compared to a theory, is a framework which derives from theory and attempts to represent reality, rather like a model of a building represents the building's parts and functions. Models provide a systematic, well-researched approach to health promotion practice.

Theories informing health promotion

As with nursing, there are a number of theories which underpin the practice of health promotion. These are informed by a multitude of academic disciplines such as **epidemiology** and **demography**, health psychology, law and ethics and politics.

Epidemiology and demography

These disciplines enable you to identify priorities and set targets (Chapters 4 and 7) based on statistical information about populations and to consider health promotion interventions suitable for a target group. For example, if the locality where you are working has a large older population with a high incidence of falls at home, you need to deliver health promotion programmes which enable them to avoid falls at home. Another example is organising child immunisation programmes if the locality has many families with young children.

Ethics and law

Ethics and law are concerned with making a series of value judgements about what health means to the individual or to the community and about whether, when and how to intervene. A central ethical question for you is what is acceptable or unacceptable. Ethics and law enable you to consider principles such autonomy, respect for the individual, freedom to make decisions without coercion, voluntary participation, confidentiality, informed consent, social justice, equity and mental capacity of patients. These principles inform you how to develop a non-discriminatory and non-judgemental practice. You need to ensure that your patient is changing behaviour on a voluntary basis and by exercising free will. For example if a smoker, after receiving health education on the risks of smoking and accessibility and availability of smoking cessation programmes decides to continue smoking then you have to accept that he exercises his free will and choice without blaming for failure to conform, known as **victim blaming**.

Your practice can be informed by the theory of beneficence and non-maleficence. It means that your health promotion interventions promote good and also prevent, remove and avoid harm to your patients. This theory places the common (majority) good before individual considerations. An example is fluoridisation of drinking water supplies to promote dental health. This is beneficial to the majority even though it may not further benefit a minority.

Health psychology theories

Health psychology is a subdivision of psychology that seeks to explain how people behave in relation to their health. In promoting health we are interested in how people change to healthy behaviours. There are many individual theories to explain this, briefly explained below.

Theories of reasoned action and planned behaviour (Ajzen and Fishbein, 1980)

These theories increase understanding of the factors that influence people's intention to behave in a certain way, which in turn enables you to develop interventions that meet individuals' needs, for example the use of **peer education**.

The health belief model (Becker, 1974)

This model demonstrates that behaviour change is dependent upon the individual's belief about their susceptibility to a disease, severity of the illness, and the cost and benefit analysis involved in any change of behaviour. Becker's health belief model enables you to understand and predict why individuals will or will not participate in different prevention activities such as health screening programmes.

The health locus of control theory (Rotter, 1966)

This theory explains the extent to which people feel that they have control over events and how their personalities are shaped as a result of these beliefs. The theory suggests that people who feel in control of their lives (**internal** locus) are more likely to change their behaviour than people who feel powerless (**external** locus).

The social cognitive theory (Bandura, 1977)

This provides a framework for understanding, predicting and changing behaviour. Bandura explored the concept of **self-efficacy** or the belief an individual has in their ability to change or overcome difficulties. He claimed that human behaviour change is governed by the following principles:

- self-efficacy: an individual's confidence to carry out a certain behaviour;
- expectancy: the belief that certain action will result in the desired outcome;
- incentives: that behaviour is guided by the value the individual places on the perceived outcome.

This will vary with different situations, for example a smoker may be confident that they can resist smoking when other people smoke at work but may be less confident that they can do this when in the pub socialising with smoker friends.

Overall, health psychology theories provide you with a sound understanding of human behaviour based on attitudes, beliefs, values, power and control, which can be used to help people change from risky behaviour and to adopt healthy behaviour by making healthier choices. However, reliance solely on behaviour change is restrictive and has been criticised as 'victim blaming' for placing the onus of change solely on the individual.

All these theories from other disciplines inform health promotion theory construction, just as theories from psychology, sociology, ethics and medicine all inform nursing theory. The next section looks at two models developed for planning health promotion initiatives: the first is a strategic planning model for community health promotion and the second is a model for encouraging behaviour change in individuals and groups.

Health promotion models

There are a variety of models which are informed by different theoretical perspectives such as health psychology; most acknowledge the need to improve health through education, prevention of illness and promotion of positive wellness. Some models emphasise one aspect or another but most can be adapted to incorporate thinking about the broader aspects of health improvement and address the Ottawa Charter principles and inequalities in health (Marmot, 2010).

Tannahill's (1985) model gives an overview of the three main organisational aspects of health promotion (see Chapter 2 for further explanation). It presupposes that health education has existed for many years, in schools for children, and for adults mainly through health professionals and the media. It acknowledges the historical and current importance of preventive services in public health, such as immunisation and screening. In addition, following the WHO imperative to generate healthy policies, the model incorporates policy-making as its third part. The whole can be seen as a very useful planning device for health promotion practice – educating about smoking, screening for smoking-related diseases and setting no-smoking policies. You can use this model as a thinking tool to imagine the whole of what you can set up as you plan health promotion for one patient, for groups of patients or for communities.

Disease prevention traditionally can be categorised into three different levels. This is useful for thinking of the scope of preventive services and strategies.

- Primary prevention: targets healthy people and aims to empower them to continue their healthy status, for example by the uptake of flu vaccination.

- Secondary prevention: targets people who are at risk of developing ill health, aiming to persuade them to seek screening, i.e. cervical screening.
- Tertiary prevention: targets unhealthy people, aiming to empower them through self-management of their illness, for example comply with medication taking.

Prochaska and DiClemente's (1982) model is one which incorporates many aspects of health psychology (see Chapter 2 for further explanation). This model was developed to explain how individuals move towards adopting behaviour that will maintain good health. It uses stages of changes as its core construct and integrates processes and principles of change derived from different theories, hence it is called 'trans-theoretical'. The model presumes the individual will go through stages of changing health behaviour which are cyclical and show that having completed one change, the person may well go on to feel that they can make another.

- At first the individual does not think of making a change – 'I'm OK as I am' – perhaps influenced by health belief and attribution theory.
- Then something may happen to make them he/she about it – 'Maybe I should do something about it'. The influence here could be what others say (social cognitive theory).
- Having made a tentative decision, the individual then wonders how to make the change – 'I'll look into it'. Internal locus of control is becoming stronger.
- The individual engages in a new behaviour, trying it out.
- Sustaining the change over time takes inner strength. Social support and self-efficacy help with this stage.
- At any time in the cycle the individual may revert to unhealthy behaviour. Health psychology and health promotion models may explain some aspects of behaviour, but do not expect them to solve the problem!

There are other models and theories of health promotion and public health to be found in the literature. We have chosen to focus on these two examples, but encourage you to read around the subject and to think about which model or theory is being used when you read about health promotion initiatives (see Further reading at the end of this chapter).

Chapter summary

This chapter has enabled you to develop an understanding of the health promotion concept, its origin and development in the UK up to the present day. It has explained how the perceived concept of health by patients and health professionals can influence health outcomes. The WHO views health promotion as instrumental in achieving global health and has identified nurses as key players who, working in partnership with others, can have a positive impact on health improvement. The WHO states that nurses can achieve this by acting as patients' **advocates**, mediators and enablers.

The promotion of positive health is the mutual responsibility of the individual, who has to take responsibility for his/her own health by adopting healthy behaviour, and of the state, which also has responsibility through the development and implementation of national and local health policies to address the wider determinants of health in order to

continued opposite...

continued...

improve the health status of the nation.

The chapter has examined different health promotion theories and models which enable you, as a nurse, to plan and implement health promotion within your nursing practice in order to empower patients to achieve optimum health.

Activities: Brief outline answers

Activity 1.1 (page 8)

- Physical: no, Abdul is not physically healthy as he has cancer and diabetes. However, according to Abdul he is physically healthy as he feels well and he is in remission. He is able to walk and go to work.
- Emotional: yes, he has the ability to recognise his emotions, i.e. fear of death.
- Intellectual: yes, he is healthy as he has the capacity to think clearly and coherently. He can make decisions about his personal affairs. He can do his work.
- Sexual: yes, he has an intimate and loving relationship with his partner.
- Social: yes, he is healthy as he has a strong friendship circle.
- Spiritual: yes, he reads the Qur'an and he has a religious faith, and considers himself spiritually healthy, a view shared by his family and colleagues.

Overall then, although his health professionals and his work colleagues may say he is not, Abdul considers himself to be healthy.

Activity 1.2 (page 12)

All of them are health-promotion activities. Consider the range of people involved and types of activity – education, prevention measures and policies. All will educate for health, prevent disease or protect the public.

Further reading

Ogden, J (2007) *Health Psychology: a textbook*, 4th edn. Milton Keynes: Open University Press.
A good review of health psychology theory and research.

Naidoo, J and Wills, J (2010) *Developing Practice for Public Health and Health Promotion*, 3rd edn. Oxford: Elsevier.
A good overview of health promotion which also explains a range of health promotion models.

Chapter 2
Tackling lifestyle change

NMC Standards for Pre-registration Nursing Education

This chapter will address the following competencies:

Domain 1: Professional values

1. All nurses must practise with confidence according to *The code: Standards of conduct, performance and ethics for nurses and midwives* (NMC 2008), and within other recognised ethical and legal frameworks. They must be able to recognise and address ethical challenges relating to people's choices and decision-making about their care, and act within the law to help them and their families and carers find acceptable solutions.

Domain 2: Communication and interpersonal skills

6. All nurses must take every opportunity to encourage health-promoting behaviour through education, role modelling and effective communication.

NMC Essential Skills Clusters

This chapter will address the following ESCs:

Cluster: Organisational aspects of care

9. People can trust the newly registered graduate nurse to treat them as partners and work with them to make a holistic and systematic assessment of their needs; to develop a personalised plan that is based on mutual understanding and respect for their individual situation promoting health and well-being, minimising risk of harm and promoting their safety at all times.

By the second progression point:

3. Understands the concept of public health and the benefits of healthy lifestyles and the potential risks involved with various lifestyles or behaviours, for example, substance misuse, smoking, obesity.

4 Recognises indicators of unhealthy lifestyles.

By entry to the register:

18. Discusses sensitive issues in relation to public health and provides appropriate advice and guidance to individuals, communities and populations, for example, contraception, substance misuse, smoking, obesity.

Cluster: Nutrition and fluid management

27. People can trust the newly registered graduate nurse to assist them to choose a diet that provides an adequate nutritional and fluid intake.

continued opposite...

continued...

By entry to the register:

6. Uses knowledge of dietary, physical, social and psychological factors to inform practice, being aware of those that can contribute to poor diet, cause or be caused by ill health.
7. Supports people to make appropriate choices and changes to eating patterns, taking account of dietary preferences, religious and cultural requirements, treatment requirements and special diets needed for health reasons.
9. Discusses in a non-judgemental way how diet can improve health and the risks associated with not eating appropriately.

Chapter aims

By the end of this chapter you will be able to:

*   locate and understand the current advice for healthy **lifestyle** choices;
*   realise the social, psychological and political dimensions of targeting lifestyle for health improvement;
*   begin working with patients on making healthy lifestyle choices.

Introduction

There is a confusion of information around healthy lifestyle choices. Some are well evidenced and clear and others seem to be difficult because the messages keep altering. As a nurse you need to have an overall understanding in order not only to guide patients when their lifestyles are causing ill health but also to answer questions from patients and the public about healthy lifestyles generally. The NMC requires that all nurses support their patients' decision-making and healthy lifestyle choices. You need to keep up to date with research evidence as it is presented through professional guidelines and campaign messages to the public. Obviously as a professional, you need to understand the evidence behind these guidelines and messages in order to become a better practitioner with more credibility with patients and the public.

Case study: Choosing a healthy lifestyle is not easy

A district nurse was visiting an elderly diabetic patient at her home when the husband of the patient suddenly said he had starting eating olive oil spread because of the reports of it possibly lowering cholesterol levels in the blood. His wife joined in with the comment that he should be eating another particular spread (containing plant sterols) as this is advertised as definitely lowering cholesterol levels. She went on to suggest, however, that all fat is bad and he should be using only a scraping of any spread on his bread.

How did the district nurse tackle this?

*   *Firstly she asked the husband to check the percentage of olive oil in the spread he was using. This was only 10% so he conceded that this was probably not worth it.*

continued overleaf...

continued... •

- *Secondly the nurse explained that the plant sterol and plant stanol spreads have been well researched and proven to act to lower blood cholesterol.*
- *But thirdly she informed the couple that these need to be eaten in certain doses to be effective – a scraping would not be enough.*

It is not easy to make decisions about healthy lifestyles when the information is so complicated. Would you be able to help as the district nurse did?

Instead of just going straight into topic areas, this chapter offers a structure for you to think about tackling lifestyle change with patients and clients. Any healthy lifestyle topic, whether multiple (such as healthy eating) or simple (such as salt in the diet) can be approached in this way. You can apply the structural approach to your favourite topics, and use it when a new topic is needed for your practice area. Figure 2.1 shows the areas you need to think about for each healthy lifestyle topic

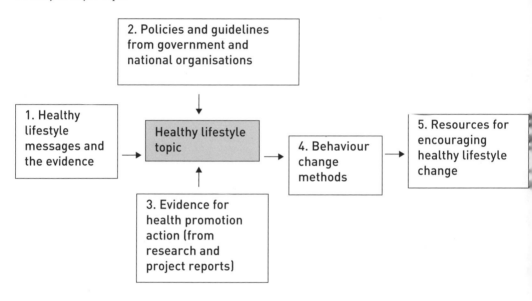

Figure 2.1: Areas to think about with healthy lifestyle topics

You need firstly to focus on and narrow down a healthy lifestyle topic. 'Sexual health' as a topic is too broad, and as a key word or phrase will give you too much information. Using more precise terminology such as 'safer sex' will narrow your search down, but 'condom use' will clearly focus more usefully. Similarly you can narrow 'obesity' down to 'exercise' or 'losing weight' and 'healthy eating' down to 'fruit and vegetables'. Try to find a single, clear behaviour change to work on with patients as, in reality, people manage change more effectively in small steps.

Once you have identified a topic, this chapter will guide you through each of the sections in boxes 1 to 5 of Figure 2.1 and explore the issues in each.

Before that, however, you need to be aware of the wider political decision-making concerned with health lifestyle choice.

The politics of healthy lifestyle choices

In modern health promotion terms there is always a tension between people making healthy choices and governments of countries providing the essential opportunities and structures for people to have choices. The WHO recognised the need to shift the emphasis away from always assuming it is the individual's responsibility towards sharing the responsibility with government-organised provision. (See Chapter 1 for details of the Ottawa Charter, which recognised the responsibility of governments to make living environments which support individual and community skills in making decisions and choices for health.) At the time in the 1980s the UK, under right-wing Conservative government rule, did not acknowledge that the state shared responsibility and tended to place responsibility on individuals for their health choices, their own health, and therefore ill health. The election of a left-wing Labour government in 1997 resulted in a health policy of shared responsibility and a focus on partnership between people and organisations and government. The government health policy in 2004 (also Labour) changed to a shift in emphasis further towards the idea of empowering people's choices by providing supportive environments. One of the clearest examples is the ban on smoking in enclosed public places, where the intent was not only to protect the public from the effects of passive smoking but also to provide better social and environmental opportunities for smokers to quit and non-smokers not to start. The public health white paper Choosing Health (Department of Health, 2004a) intended to refocus from major disease targets to lifestyle issues and to promise more central government intervention to support healthy lifestyle choices. The targets named in this white paper were: reducing the numbers of people who smoke, reducing obesity and improving diet and nutrition, increasing exercise, encouraging and supporting sensible drinking, improving sexual health and improving mental health.

In the new coalition government of Spring 2010 the Conservative and Liberal Democrat parties, right wing and centre, produced their own white paper for England, which replaces the previous one. Healthy Lives, Healthy People (Department of Health, 2010a) declares that centralisation has failed and promises a radical new approach which focuses on work in local communities, led by local government. The government intends to tackle the promotion of healthy lifestyles through recognising the difficulties and inequalities people face, and providing educational, social and financial support for people's healthy choices. The targets of this white paper are given not as topics, but as intentions to work in ways which address root causes of ill health.

Healthy lifestyle messages and the evidence

Going now to the sections of Figure 2.1, remember your chosen lifestyle topic and apply the following ideas for finding the evidence.

Interpreting the message

We tend to be bombarded from all directions by messages that tell us to do this and that, or not to do something. Have you ever tried to collect them all and put them together as a set of ideas for working with your patients, or even your own family?

Here are some of these messages you may have come across:

- eat five portions of fruit and vegetables a day;
- take enough exercise;
- eat less salt;
- use condoms;
- eat less fat overall, but particularly saturated fat;
- don't smoke at all;
- drink more water;
- wear safe shoes;
- drink a sensible level of alcohol.

But do you know the detailed instructions related to the messages, and do you know the evidence behind them?

Start with the message to eat five portions of fruit and vegetables a day. Many people were confused when this campaign started in 2003. They were asking what it meant by fruit and vegetables, whether it can include potatoes (it can't) or baked beans (it can; the tomato sauce counts). They were confused as to what a portion is (information available on **nhs.uk/Livewell/5ADAY**), and whether the fruit and vegetables all have to be different (they do, as the five different colours are the various anti-oxidant vitamins). You can see from this that there are often complicated instructions for what seems to be a simple message. Finally you need to consider why people should eat more fruit and vegetables, in order to be able to explain to others. It is now accepted evidence that anti-oxidant vitamins help to prevent the degeneration of tissues which can lead to coronary heart disease and cancers. However, it has lately been acknowledged that the five-a-day campaign has not really been effective in persuading people to eat more fruit and vegetables.

Another message which causes controversy is that for sensible drinking (alcohol). Some adults will remember that the safe number of units of alcohol suggested for men and women daily has changed over the years. They will tell you that 'the government can't make up its mind, so what does it matter?'. The recommended sensible limits are currently three to four units per day for men, and two to three units per day for women. More recently the issue of whether pregnant women can drink has been confusing – the best evidence at the moment is that no alcohol at all should be drunk during pregnancy but some researchers have an opinion that a little does not do harm; this means probably ½ to 1 unit a day. (One alcohol unit is measured as 10ml or 8g of pure alcohol. This equals one 25ml single measure of whisky (ABV 40%), or a third of a pint of beer (ABV 5–6%) or half a standard (175ml) glass of red wine (ABV 12%)). Drinking a lot of alcohol at once (binge drinking) is dangerous. It can lead to liver and brain damage, accidents and encourage violent crime. Binge drinking is considered to be drinking 6 units for women and 8 units for men, at any one time. (Further information available can be found on the website **www.drinkaware.co.uk**.)

Can you find the same level of detail for other messages?

Activity 2.1   *Research and finding evidence*

Now think of a healthy lifestyle topic to do the same investigation of the message. For example how much and what sort of exercise should a well adult be doing and why?

1. What is the message – exactly?
2. What details would someone ask about the message? How does someone follow it?
3. What is the evidence? Why are people being asked to do this? What does this choice prevent, and how?

There is an outline answer for this activity at the end of the chapter.

Finding the latest and most evidence-based message for a healthy lifestyle topic is an important part of the nurse's role in health promotion. In addition, adaptations to the message will be needed.

Adapting the message

The messages need to be adapted for everyone depending on people's wide variety of circumstances. Most campaigns are aware of this and you will find variations for children, the differently able, the elderly, etc. Perhaps not in the campaign information, but in the evidence from projects professionals have published will be variations you can apply to different groups such as those with ethnic differences, religious constraints and social disadvantages. What is not explored so well is the variation you may need for your patients with existing illnesses (both physical and mental).

Activity 2.2   *Critical thinking*

Consider a patient you are caring for (or you could just use these examples to think more generally). Find a healthy lifestyle message that would apply to them, for example eating less fat.

Draw up a list of possible variations your patient has which would mean you have to modify that message:

- age – children and older adults have different needs;
- gender – women and men may have specific issues to do with physiology or social norms;
- religion – several religions have constraints on individual choices;
- culture – people across the world have different ways of living;
- income level – this will link to social circumstance, housing and access to a healthy lifestyle;
- education level – not something we tend to measure but think about the patient's ability to learn;
- effects of illness – the patient's illness or their psychological responses to it will affect learning and the ability to change lifestyle.

Modify the message to suit.

There is an outline answer for this activity at the end of the chapter.

In addition to understanding the evidence supporting the healthy lifestyle messages, you need to consider the origins of the messages and the related guidance for their use. The next section goes on to discuss this.

Policies and guidelines from government and national organisations

This is the next section of Figure 2.1 to be considered. The UK government, its departments, agencies and partners produce policies and guidelines on all health issues. The healthy lifestyle topics sometimes appear alone (smoking) or in groups (drugs, alcohol and smoking) or integrated into disease-related strategies (coronary heart disease and cancers). The policies come in different guises. There are laws (smoking ban in public), white papers (various aspects of public health), national service frameworks (for example diabetes) and strategic plans (for example sexual health). These are usually applicable across the UK but you need to be aware of countrywide variations.

When you are looking into a healthy lifestyle topic, the Department of Health is a good place to start as they originate or commission so many of these documents (use the website **www.dh.gov. uk**). Charity organisations also produce guidelines and are reliable (for example Diabetes UK, British Heart Foundation); some are official partners with the government and take the lead (such as Drinkaware, the Terrence Higgins Trust, Breast Cancer Care). You could also just use an internet search engine to find documents on your topic – in which case you must be careful to look at the organisation name on the url and only rely on government or other official sites such as charities and professional organisations. Don't, for example, make the mistake of using a commercial company site for guidance when they are in the business of selling products. Websites set up as personal opinion and radical anti-establishment outlets can be used to make you think, but do be professional about how you use the information. Tell your patients the same thing.

Table 2.1 shows some of the current national documents which guide practice in healthy lifestyle promotion. It does not include the very useful National Health Service documents which focus on care provision but which also address some prevention issues (such as the national service frameworks).

What you must do is find the follow-up to the document you are researching. For example, notice that the current smoking document was published and put on the statutes as a white paper in 1999, and is still in force. Since then many changes have taken place, including the public smoking bans which were agreed in the white paper Choosing Health in 2004. The most recent change has been the tobacco control plan for England.

When you go into the Department of Health website, the latest news will be there and you can see that some of the most popular documents are posted on the front page. Use the website's search box to find any document you are looking for.

Lifestyle topic	Date	Guideline	Organisation
General – current public health white paper	2010	Healthy Lives, Healthy People	Department of Health
General – children	2007	Healthy Lives, Brighter Futures: The strategy for children and young people's health	Department of Health
Obesity	2008	Healthy Weight, Healthy Lives	HM Government
Healthy eating	2002	Five-a-day programme (fruit and vegetables)	Department of Health
Sexual health	2001	National Strategy for Sexual Health and HIV	Department of Health
	2010	Teenage Pregnancy Strategy: Beyond 2010	Teenage Pregnancy Unit, Department for Education
Drugs	1995	Tackling Drugs Together to Build a Better Britain	Department of Health
Smoking	1999	Smoking Kills	Department of Health
	2011	Healthy Lives, Healthy People: A tobacco control plan for England	Department of Health
Mental health	2002	National Suicide Prevention Strategy	Department of Health
Physical activity	2004	At Least Five a Week: evidence from the Chief Medical Officer	Department of Health
	2009	Be Active, Be Healthy	Department of Health
Alcohol	2004	Alcohol Harm Reduction Strategy	Department of Health

Table 2.1: National (led by England) guidelines for some healthy lifestyle topics

Activity 2.3   *Research and finding evidence*

Go to the Department of Health website. Enter 'physical activity' into the search box. Look at the documents they list:

* Change4Life;
* at least five a week;
* a follow up from the previous white paper – choosing activity;
* a challenge for NHS staff to get active.

continued overleaf...

continued... •

Some of the documents listed will inevitably be either old ones or merely press releases and letters from the Department. However, this is a useful way to find out what is published and the website puts them in order of usefulness. Put in your own healthy lifestyle topic and see what comes up.

As this activity is an exploration of what is available, there is no outline answer at the end of the chapter.

Having looked at the national strategies and guidelines for healthy lifestyle topics, you may have found some helpful ideas for practice in the examples given by the documents. Next you need to move on to the effectiveness of health promotion practice itself. The next step in the structure in Figure 2.1 is to show that your methods of practice are evidence-based.

Evidence for health promotion action

You need to find out if the health messages and the national guidelines are working. This section looks at the effectiveness of health promotion which delivers the message to improve healthy lifestyles.

Health promotion can be structured as a combination of health education, prevention services (primary, secondary and tertiary) and policies to protect health (Tannahill, 2009). These three aspects should be based on the best available evidence from research, from national campaigns and from evaluation of local practice.

Concept summary: Tannahill's (1985 and 2009) model of health promotion

This model explains Tannahill's view that health promotion is a mixture of the following three areas of activity.

- Health education – teaching people about health and how to live healthily. This is done largely through schools and the media, although as health professionals we also have a role in this.
- Prevention – providing services to prevent disease, such as immunisation, screening and support to live well with an existing disease.
- Health protection – which Tannahill sees as setting laws, policies and allocating money to promote health.

The three areas overlap with each other so that health education can help prevent disease, and health protection can agree policy for education and prevention services. The model is useful for making you think of all possible aspects of a topic – such as smoking.

1. health education in schools and by the NHS at smokefree.nhs.uk;
2. prevention through smoking cessation classes and nicotine replacement;
3. health protection from the ban on smoking in enclosed public places and restrictions on advertising and sales.

The model shows the interrelationships between teaching people about healthy lifestyles (health education), understanding what is being prevented and how (prevention) and the policy environment in which choices are made (health protection). Tannahill's model enables health professionals to think of a whole approach to health promotion for groups of people with similar needs. Now apply Tannahill's model to your work with people on healthy lifestyles.

Activity 2.4   *Critical thinking*

Think of how health promotion can be constructed for a healthy lifestyle topic, for example oral health.

- Health education – what would you teach patients?
- Prevention services – what would you advise patients to do about preventing disease? Who could help them?
- What can you find out about protective policies and national guidelines?

There is an outline answer for this activity at the end of the chapter.

The model, as you can see, attempts to cover the potential whole range of initiatives to improve health: educating people, providing prevention services and setting policies to protect health. It should enable you to plan interventions across that range within your practice.

Many local health promotion initiatives are also structured around these three aspects, even though they may not say so. Local initiatives (often called projects) are set up on one or more topics, for example tackling obesity in children, foot health for the elderly, healthy eating for long-term mentally ill people or a youth-focused project tackling a mixture of alcohol, drugs, sex and safety in the street. This kind of work gives evidence which is not from scientific research, but is seen as collecting evidence from interventions and is usually evaluated with collections of data which are a mixture of quantitative and qualitative responses.

Evidence for health promotion is often not strong. Research using randomised controlled trials (the best sort of evidence) is rarely conducted in the case of setting up an initiative involving for example sex education classes or after-school sports, or campaigns on using less salt. They are difficult because different groups have to be organised so that a strict comparison can be made when the only difference between them is the intervention itself. Imagine having two groups of children in a school where one group has swimming classes and one does not. The children in the non-swimming group may go swimming with their families, so the difference is lost. Also, it would be seen as unfair and ethically unjustifiable to deprive one group of an intervention when it is known to be beneficial. Imagine a group of obese children in one community, where half of them join a special exercise class and the other half get no extra help.

Clearly there are some instances where strictly scientific research methods could work: nicotine replacement therapy, cancer screening, weight loss programmes for adults. The ethical issues remain but at least the intervention itself can be controlled. Some researches compare two or more interventions such as different diets. The National Institute for Health and Clinical Excellence (NICE) has published the best evidence for a range of public health topics (as well as the better known work they do on drug treatments). To find these documents go to the NICE website, **www.nice.org.uk**, and look for your topic or look at the list of public health guidelines. There is a general document on behaviour change (NICE, 2007).

Finding out whether any national or local health promotion initiatives are effective can be difficult as the evaluations are not well disseminated. National campaigns should publish their information: what the aims were, how the campaign has evolved and what the results have been. A good example is the long-running No Smoking Day campaign, on **www.nosmokingday. org.uk**, where you can find details in their publications. They declare for instance that one in ten smokers made an attempt to quit smoking on No Smoking Day 2009 – a good result, achieved through massive media work and events held across the country.

Local projects in health promotion are often harder to find. Some edited textbooks will have chapters written by people who report on their project; some journals will have articles similarly written. Any local community health organisation works with their local authority to generate and operate local initiatives to improve health. Note that, at the time of publication, a reorganisation of local health provision is in progress. The coalition government proposes to have local authorities deliver public health when they remove the Primary Care Trusts in England. Try looking up your local authority website to see what projects have been reported or are ongoing.

Finally, a scholarly approach should lead you into doing a literature search using search engines and journal databases. What you will find is a good and wide professional literature on health promotion research and health promotion intervention projects/initiatives. You will need to refine your keywords to narrow your search to the most relevant articles. See the further reading list at the end of this chapter for a good reference to searching for information.

Having by this time found out the details of the health messages, looked at the national guidelines around them and read some evidence from projects in the literature, you are now ready to plan interventions for your patients. The next section examines ways to change behaviour.

Behaviour change methods

All health promotion can be seen as having the aim of promoting **health behaviour** change. Even when using Tannahill's model, it is about:

- education to promote behaviour change;
- promoting a change to preventive behaviour and using preventive services;
- being aware of the effect of social and environmental constraints on change and also the promotion of healthy choices through healthy policy setting.

Behaviour change models

No-one makes choices or changes behaviour in isolation. There are internal factors such as their upbringing, influences on beliefs and attitudes from general education, culture and family. There are external factors such as environment, social contacts, religion and income. How people make health behaviour changes has been the subject of much theory and research. There are models of behaviour change which are based on beliefs and knowledge (cognition models), social influence (social cognition models) and empowerment (empowerment models), all of which are helpful for you to consider in order to help patients change their behaviour.

Cognition models focus on the thinking of the individual, so their beliefs, attitudes and values are most influential in their decision-making. This will mean that as a nurse you work with their beliefs or work to change their beliefs, either to help a patient to develop a way of adapting the health message (losing weight on a personal choice of preferred food) or convince them to alter their beliefs (to try a different way of eating from that 'set' by family or bad experiences perhaps).

Social cognition models introduce the influence of other people on a patient's behaviour, so that the patient may worry about not being 'normal' or being seen to be 'fussy' or 'picky' if they choose things their friends would not. Men giving up drinking alcohol may be ridiculed by their mates for choosing a 'girly' soft drink. Sometimes the fear factor is strong, either stopping health behaviour (fear of looking fat in an exercise class) or promoting the behaviour (reading about famous young women dying of cervical cancer may encourage attendance for smear tests).

Empowerment models (see also Chapter 5) make the assumption that the previous two types of behaviour change theories do not take into account how hard it is for people to make decisions to change. Empowerment theories show how people need to become empowered through their own previous actions (they learn how to be successful) or need to be empowered by others – in this case by you as a nurse. The NMC standards include the role of the nurse in empowering patients in their decision-making. Empowerment does not come because more knowledge is gained, so giving your patient all the information will only go so far. Empowerment is also about being able to weigh up or judge the information – empowering the patient to decide for themselves, even when new or conflicting information is released. Further, empowerment is boosting the patient's own belief in his/her abilities to make decisions. You know yourself how difficult this is when other people do not believe that you can do it. Not least, empowerment is about 'making space' for the patient, ensuring his/her voice is heard and their opinions valued. Some would call this a true partnership with the patient.

A model of behaviour change which purports to cross over and include all the theories above is the transtheoretical stages of change model (Prochaska and DiClemente, 1982), see Table 2.2. The idea is that people go through stages and the health professional can enable progress through these stages. It is important to realise that this alters the way a nurse can enable behaviour change. It is foolish to simplistically imagine that the patient will start to change as soon as he/she has had a teaching session on the ward or in the practice, and then take on board the goal of change such as giving up smoking. The authors of the model suggest that the goal of a health professional given their limited time with each patient need only be to move the patient from one stage to the next, since expecting to complete the cycle any time soon is unrealistic.

The model describes how people go through stages where at first they do not consider changing their health behaviour (pre-contemplation), then start to think they should (contemplation). The next stage is to get ready to change by reading and investigating how to change (preparation), followed by taking the first step in trying a new behaviour (making a change). At several stages, people may relapse and go back to old behaviours, commonly when they have tried something and it has not worked for them. Eventually though, the model describes how people maintain a new healthy behaviour and stay changed. Each stage is not easy to reach from the previous one and how you as a nurse can help is in finding ways to motivate someone to take another step along the model or back into the process from a relapse.

Stage of change	What happens	Moving someone to the next stage
Pre-contemplation	The patient is unaware that a change is needed and/or has no intention of changing in the future.	Something to attract and alert the patient is required. Perhaps a fun event with a free gift or a graphic fear-inducing warning.
Contemplation	Some realisation is occurring and the patient expresses that 'I really ought to do this – sometime.'	The patient needs to be helped to make a plan. The idea that there are many ways of changing can be introduced. Sometimes the story of a successful role model can help: 'If he can do it, so can I.'
Preparing to change	Now the patient is seeking information about changing, asking questions, reading about it. Not changing yet though, still looking for support and reassurance.	Without causing information overload, ideas are required. Provide a range of options, and a range of sources of information – leaflets, websites, free introductory sessions. Encourage the choice of something to try out. Negotiate a start date, or the investigation will take a long time.
Making a change	The decision is made to try a new way to make a change. It may be quite tentative and dependent on the weather or who goes to the group. The change is tried out; for a while it will be seen as a test period.	Now is the time for praise and building self-esteem. Listen to the patient as they describe their experience of change. Congratulate them and encourage them to keep it up. At the same time you can reassure them that one slip up does not mean failure.
Relapse	This does not always happen. The patient does not like what they are trying out – 'it doesn't work', 'I don't like it', 'they were not nice to me'.	This is the potential failure. Work with the patient on what to do next. It may be that he/she needs to try an entirely new method as this one did not suit. It may be that he/she only needs to be told again that one day of bad behaviour does not mean that they cannot start again.

continued opposite...

continued...

| Staying changed | The particular new health behaviour has been established. The patient is convinced it is working, in fact they become rather proud and tell everybody. | The job is not finished yet. The patient now needs to complete his/her empowerment. They are successful and need praise; they need to use their new power. Try asking them to speak to other patients about their success. Ask them for suggestions for helping other patients. |
| On to the next change? This model is an upward climbing spiral. | The successful, empowered patient tries a change in another aspect of their health. | |

Table 2.2: Prochaska and DiClemente's stages of change model
Adapted from Prochaska and DiClemente (1982)

Activity 2.5   *Communication*

Consider a patient from the following list:

- a 50-year-old woman with diabetes;
- a 30-year-old man with a personality disorder;
- a 14-year-old girl with asthma;
- a 24-year-old man who has a learning disability.

How would you work with them on their smoking cessation at each stage of the Prochaska and DiClemente model?

There is an outline answer for this activity at the end of the chapter.

Understanding and using these behaviour change models may help you to understand how theory can work in practice. Seeing how people progress from one stage of the stages of change model to another will enable you to set realistic goals in health promotion, rather than expecting immediate new health behaviour.

Behaviour change techniques

In addition to the behaviour change models above, there are other techniques that you might want to consider using. These have been developed mainly within the medical profession as tools for use by general practitioners and of course other health professionals have adopted their use.

Motivational interviewing (Rollnick et al., 2008) is an interpersonal style rather than a structured model. It has four general principles:

1. express empathy with the problem and the need to change;
2. develop discrepancy (make people understand the differences and the advantages and disadvantages) between current behaviour and desired change;
3. accept resistance to change as normal;
4. support self-efficacy and autonomy in changing behaviour.

In this way motivational interviewers can show the patient that their problem is understandable, their need to change is evident, that reluctance to change is natural and that the patient can do it. Motivational interviewing tends to stand alone as a technique and is used very often by medical professionals. The goal is often to empower, and as a nurse you can adopt the technique as a means to show the patient the same things.

Brief intervention (Babor and Higgins-Biddle, 2001) is a term used to indicate the time available and taken, rather than any particular technique. It can also be referred to as solution-focused brief therapy and is intended to keep the session directly on the issue of the behaviour change needed. Most of the writers in this field suggest that it has the following principles:

1. raise awareness of the risks in current behaviour;
2. emphasise the patient's responsibility in making a change;
3. give advice to change;
4. make suggestions for strategies for change;
5. encourage goal-setting and action planning for change.

Brief intervention can be the focus used in any of the previous theories and models, as a means to take the patient quite quickly to a decision point and action. It is used very often in alcohol behaviour and emotional issues. It is slightly more direct than motivational interviewing and tends to challenge the patient to action. The goal is to make change happen soon, as the risks are high.

A totally different approach to health behaviour change has been recently re-introduced to the debate. Financial incentives to change behaviour have been proposed particularly in the areas of obesity and weight loss. In a scheme backed by the National Health Service called Weight Wins, run by a private company, people are offered cash for losing pounds and for keeping them off. There have been suggestions for using incentives in other topics such as compliance with drug treatments, contraception uptake, screening attendance and smoking cessation. The incentives need not be cash, but could be vouchers for food or donations to charities.

The NICE is unsure about the effectiveness of incentives and has set up a consultation around the issue. They feel that their use could be divisive, rewarding people for what should be done anyway and unfair to people who do it by themselves. People who argue for the use of incentives feel that any method of improving health is worthwhile.

Resources for encouraging healthy lifestyle change

The final step in Figure 2.1 is for you to think of resources in your chosen topic.

Now you have a better idea of the messages you want to deliver, the policy background, evidence for health promotion and ways to address behaviour change, you need to consider what resources to use with patients. You can, to an extent, rely on your own knowledge and skills to explain, to write instructions, to draw diagrams and so on. However, there are many sources of useful teaching materials to help you and to provide for the patients and clients to use for themselves.

Firstly, think of what sort of resource material would be useful to your patient group and care environment.

- Leaflets are reading material and not everyone reads, or they may learn better through other means.
- Posters can have impact and may attract the attention of people at pre-contemplation stage. They can make an interesting and eye-catching display.
- Websites that the patients can access are becoming more useful. Children are particularly computer aware and 'silver surfers' are on the increase.
- Films on DVD are ideal for a group session or for continual showing in a waiting area.
- Models of parts of the body, food portion sizes, lungs damaged by smoking, etc., can make things clearer than a diagram. Equipment such as tape measures indicating healthy waist size, pedometers, condom demonstrator models can all be found.
- Increasingly, mobile phone 'apps' are being used, which are on the increase from commercial companies working with slimming for example, and there is a British Heart Foundation recipe finder free from iTunes.
- Finally, when you are teaching a group about a healthy lifestyle, try to make it fun and give free gifts such as apples, toothbrushes and smiley face badges.

Remember that all teaching resource materials are more effective when accompanied by health professional input. Work with your patient to personalise the resource. See Chapter 4 for more information and advice on teaching patients.

You need to understand where to get resources from. Again, as at the beginning of the chapter, think of a health message and locate organisations which produce related resources.

Activity 2.6   *Research and finding evidence*

Using the '5 a Day' message, contact your local community health organisation, which has the remit to provide resources to everyone in the area working on health.

- Is there a government official organisation for this topic?
- Is there a day or week or month for the topic across the country or the world?
- Is there a charity organisation which is involved (it will probably not be exactly on the healthy lifestyle topic, but on a related preventable disease).
- Is there a commercial organisation which you can officially ask for help? Be careful here because you do not want to advertise and you must not go outside your employer's purchasing contracts.
- What resources can you get free? What is the cost involved if not?

There is an outline answer for this activity at the end of the chapter.

There are many possible sources of resources for health promotion, but you will have to work at obtaining them, as they are not located conveniently. Further guidance on managing resources in practice is given in Chapter 7.

Having looked at all the sections on the original structure in Figure 2.1, you should have a good idea of how to put together information and methods for healthy lifestyle topics. Consider the topic you chose at the beginning of the chapter: think of the evidence for the message, the policies involved, the evidence for health promotion being done, the behaviour change methods you can use and finally the resources available. One area left to explore is that of the nurse's own healthy lifestyle choices.

Nurses as healthy role models

The Prime Minister's 2010 commission on the future of nursing and midwifery reported that nurses should be role models for healthy living, and take responsibility for their own health. The International Council of Nurses made a similar statement on International Nurses Day in 2010.

There were various responses to the statements, mostly agreeing with the need to be healthy but refuting the idea of role modelling as it may be seen as pretending to be better than the patient. Imagine what the patient may feel being helped by a nurse who shows extremely healthy behaviour – admiration or inferiority, aspiration or defeat? It is interesting that this imperative to become a role model is often directed at health professionals whereas it would be unusual to expect a teacher never to have failed an exam or a counsellor never to have had an emotional problem. Perhaps we should recognise that nurses are as imperfect as anyone else and that what they can role model is not perfect behaviour but the ability to find things out, to be doing something about it and to be aware of risks.

Take smoking for example: if you are a smoker the patient can either relate to you or say that you can't help them. If you are a non-smoker the patient can either emulate you or say you don't know what it's like. If you are a smoker who has quit, the patient may either admire you or say it was easier for you for some reason. The point is that you can and should be able to help a smoker to begin to quit whatever your personal behaviour. What you can model is having the facts and understanding the risks and knowing where to get help.

Chapter summary

This chapter has explored the issues involved in nurses working to promote health through tackling change towards healthy lifestyles. There are several themes under discussion, including the political dimension to healthy lifestyle, the difficulty of finding the evidence and the support needed for people to change behaviour. The role of nurses has been coordinated into a structure which is designed to help you gather the information you need to work with healthy lifestyle topics. This structure includes the understanding of healthy lifestyle messages, national policies, evidence for effective health promotion, health behaviour change and resources to help you help your patients.

Activities: brief outline answers

Activity 2.1 (page 27)

The exercise message is 'at least five a week', meaning the following:

- At least 30 minutes a day of at least moderate intensity physical activity on five or more days of the week. This can be one session or several short sessions of at least 10 minutes, or structured sessions of sports for example. All exercise helps with weight management; for bone health, activities that produce high physical stresses on the bones are necessary. This will help to protect against cardiovascular disease, cancer, type 2 diabetes and obesity.
- Older adults should take particular care to keep moving through daily activity and do specific activities to improve strength, coordination and balance.
- Children and young people should achieve a total of at least 60 minutes of at least moderate intensity physical activity each day. At least twice a week this should include activities to improve bone health (activities that produce high physical stresses on the bones), muscle strength and flexibility. This helps to prevent risk factors for disease, avoidance of weight gain, achieving a high peak bone mass, and mental wellbeing.

Activity 2.2 (page 27)

The message is eat less fat, especially saturated fat – no more than 30g a day for men and 20g a day for women.

- Children should have less saturated fat than adults. But a low fat diet isn't suitable for children under five as they need the nutrients. Older people who are frail or underweight should not have a low fat diet either.
- Some methods of cooking are traditionally high fat using for example ghee (clarified butter) or palm oil, both of which are saturated fats.
- When a family has a low income they tend to choose the cheaper supermarket food and the easy ready-made food. This limited set of choices is usually high in fat.
- Have you tried to work out from the labels how much fat is in your food? Labels give either a gram weight of fat or a percentage. However, you also have to work out the total fat and the saturated fat. This requires a level of reading and mathematical ability.
- People trying to lower their blood cholesterol are advised to lower total fats and saturated fats in their diets. There is currently much controversy as to whether a weight-reducing diet should be low fat or low carbohydrate. A very low fat diet can lead to poor levels of hormones and affect fertility and brain function.

Activity 2.4. (page 31)

Health education:

- teaching knowledge of teeth and gum health and disease – fluoride, acid foods;
- demonstrating practice of flossing, brushing and tongue cleaning;
- enabling behaviour change by motivating and empowering.

Preventive services:

- fluoride added to tap water;
- regular visits to dentist;
- self-screening bleeding gums, pain, signs of cavities.

Protective guidelines:

- Do you know if your local water is fluoridised?

- Should you use fluoride toothpaste? Should a child?
- The British Dental Association now recommends using straws with fizzy drinks, not rinsing after using fluoride toothpaste, and ending a meal with alkaline food such as cheese, not fruit.

Activity 2.5 (page 35)

There will probably be more similarities than differences between these people. Each of them may have fears, a lack of awareness and a varying level of ability to make a decision. This shows some ideas of the more likely variations as follows.

Pre-contemplation

- Older people may resent being told what to do and may rely on traditional ways or think they know things because they are experienced. Having illnesses just means getting older and causes more resentment. They may not respond well to having to read more or expose their problems in a group.
- People with mental illness often have no insight into the risks they are running. They can be inattentive and unresponsive to advice. Habitual behaviours such as smoking are frequently part of the whole make-up of the person, and may be multiple (alcohol and drugs perhaps as well).
- Teenagers tend to resent having to manage long-term illness. They also cannot see the point of health advice for what they see as 'old people's illnesses'. Smoking may be 'cool' in their group and the opinion of their peers is very influential. Some ways of quitting are more difficult than others; going to a group where they are all adults is not very encouraging. Try to find age-appropriate learning materials. Using rewards is popular in this age group.
- For people with learning disabilities, the approach needs to be at the appropriate cognitive level: for example, simple messages, demonstrations which are close to reality, and clear associations of cigarettes with coughing. Metaphors and stylised material are not easily understood. Supervision and guidance is vital as attention may vary and repetition of your input will be needed.

When dealing with the stages, these differences can interfere with your work. Some patients will take much longer than others to go from stage to stage and the final goal of quitting smoking may not be attained.

Activity 2.6 (page 37)

- An allocation of free government leaflets and posters may be available locally. There will also be a lending service for some audiovisual resources and food models. Also ask the dieticians if they can help.
- Go to **www.nhs.uk/livewell/5aday**. Leaflets cards and materials for children are available from the Department of Health website – publications. This is a good website to teach a patient from: you could guide them through it.
- There is no specific fruit and vegetable event. Try National Heart Month and World Cancer Day. Find the calendar on **www.equip.nhs.uk/Events/EventList.aspx**.
- The British Heart Foundation and the World Cancer Research Fund are very much involved with giving advice on the benefits of eating fruit and vegetables. Resources may cost though.
- Your care organisation's catering company would be a good place to start. They may be persuaded to donate fruit or sponsor activities. Similarly, local traders and markets may like to be associated with you.

Further reading

Ogden, J (2007) *Health Psychology: a textbook*, 4th edn. Milton Keynes: Open University Press.
A good basic review of a wide range of health behaviour change theories with critical comments about their effective applications.

Hutchfield, K (2010) *Information Skills for Nursing Students*. Exeter: Learning Matters.
A good instruction book for using information technology.

Useful websites

www.dh.gov.uk/en/index.htm
Department of Health website: good for using their search engine to look up topics, it will take you to their recent publications.

http://guidance.nice.org.uk/
National Institute for Health and Clinical Excellence, where you can find the best evidence for health promotion interventions as collated so far.

www.talktofrank.com/
The current drugs awareness organisation. Useful for information on all recreational drugs and resources for use in practice.

www.drinkaware.co.uk/facts
The site for alcohol information and the national campaign.

www.nhs.uk/Pages/HomePage.aspx
The public access page of the NHS current 'choice agenda' created by the labour government in 2008. This is where people are directed to in public libraries.

Chapter 3
Encouraging health screening

:::: NMC Standards for Pre-registration Nursing Education

This chapter will address the following competencies:

Domain 3: Nursing practice and decision-making

5. All nurses must understand public health principles, priorities and practice in order to
   recognise and respond to the major causes and social determinants of health, illness
   and health inequalities. They must use a range of information and data to assess the
   needs of people, groups, communities and populations and work to improve health,
   wellbeing and experiences of healthcare; secure equal access to health screening,
   health promotion and health care and promote social inclusion.

Chapter aims

By the end of this chapter you will be able to:

- give an account of screening for ill health, as part of secondary prevention of ill health
  within health promotion;
- understand the importance of health screening;
- identify and list the range of the screening types available in the UK;
- recognise how nurses may be able to discuss health screening with patients.

Introduction

Screening is the process of undertaking particular tests on apparently healthy, symptom-free
people, who may be at risk of a specific disease or condition of which they are unaware. This
testing of people is carried out on a large scale and people are invited from particular age or
gender groups.

As a nurse you need to have an understanding of how members of the population will be offered
the chance to have health screening and what kinds of screening are available in the UK. You
must be aware of how this could make a contribution to their health and wellbeing and you
should be able to answer questions that some of your patients may have. Nurses must also be
aware about some of the reasons patients may choose whether or not to accept the invitation for
screening. The subject of screening is regularly discussed in the media, and some health issues
can be given a high profile. Patients may turn to you to discuss the various topics, in which case
you need to have a clear understanding of the guidelines behind the screening programmes.
This chapter considers the role of health promotion and screening. It aims to give an account

of the screening programmes currently available to all ages in the UK. The national screening programme does not screen for all diseases, however, and nurses need to be aware of this.

Health promotion and health screening

The role of health promotion in secondary prevention of ill health is to raise awareness of screening programmes available, to encourage people to attend and take up the invitations extended to them and to support and help with understanding the results of the screening. Or, it may be that people need to be encouraged to go for testing at the first sign of a health problem. By finding out if the disease is present at an early stage, appropriate early treatment can make a successful outcome more likely. Secondary prevention involves action to seek out disease at an early stage followed by intervention during the early stages of the disease to prevent further damage. The action that is carried out is screening, allowing for treatment to commence at much earlier stages.

Concept summary: Disease prevention is at three levels

Primary prevention

Action to keep people healthy and free from disease, e.g. encouragement of healthy lifestyle, immunisation.

Secondary prevention

Action to identify disease in people, which they can be unaware of, e.g. screening.

Tertiary prevention

Actions taken to promote recovery or prevent further disability once a disease has developed, e.g. rehabilitation, advice on use of medicines, advice on lifestyle changes, support to live well with the disease.

Screening therefore has the potential to save lives, or improve the quality of life, by the process of early detection or diagnosis of serious conditions and encouraging people to seek treatment at the first sign of a health problem.

It is not a foolproof process, however; screening reduces the risk of development or further development of an existing condition (which may have complications), but it cannot give guarantees of protection. Not all health issues are suitable for screening. Any decision to develop large-scale screening programmes will involve collecting a great deal of medical evidence and consideration of the ethical issues. Health promotion must also include an advocacy function, to encourage informed public debate and discussion as policies evolve for large scale screening programmes.

There are occasions in any screening programme where there will be a number of results wrongly reporting some people as having the condition. This is referred to as false positives, and wrong reports of not having the condition are called false negatives. It is important that there are realistic expectations of what a screening programme has to offer. The UK National Screening Committee is increasingly presenting screening as risk reduction, not risk elimination, thus emphasising the limitations (NSC, 2010). Screening can reduce the risk of developing a condition or the complications of that condition; however, it cannot offer guarantees of protection.

National screening programmes

The NHS in the UK organises screening for a range of health problems and conditions throughout life. From antenatal and newborn screening programmes, with testing carried out at set times, to childhood, mid-life and later-life screening. As a nurse you may not find yourself directly involved in practice with patients undergoing all the screening tests, but you must know enough to understand and answer patients' questions.

Antenatal and newborn screening

NHS antenatal screening includes ultrasound imaging, and tests for Down's syndrome, sickle cell, thalassemia, foetal anomaly, and infectious diseases (HIV, hepatitis B, syphilis and rubella). The screening programme aims to offer testing and information to all pregnant women. NHS newborn screening involves testing hearing, newborn physical examination and the bloodspot programme. The bloodspot programme in England will offer screening for congenital hypothyroidism (CHT), phenylketonuria (PKU), sickle cell disease disorders (SCD), cystic fibrosis (CF) and medium-chain acyl-CoA dehydrogenase deficiency (MCADD). Some parts of the country will offer different tests. For regional variations check the individual websites, for example Scotland and Northern Ireland, England and Wales (NSC, 2010). Childhood screening continues with the school entry health check, where three separate elements are checked at about four to five years of age. With parental consent, growth and height are monitored. An audiologist carries out a hearing assessment and an orthoptist will assess vision.

To get a good idea of all the available screening tests offered throughout the decades of life, it is useful to consult the NHS screening timeline for the UK, found at the National Screening Committee website (**http://webarchive.nationalarchives.gov.uk/20100407120 701/screening.nhs.uk/**).

Mid-life and later life screening

For mid-life and later life screening, national cancer screening programmes in the UK exist for breast, cervical and bowel cancer. Where screening for cancer is possible, it is a key tool in detecting abnormalities at early stages. This allows treatment to be started when the cancer has the best chance of being cured, or in some cases even before it develops (DH, 2010b). When considering cancer screening in the UK, it is important to remember that each country within the UK (England and Wales, Scotland and Northern Ireland) will each have their individual screening programmes. There may be slight differences in age ranges for invitation to attend the screening. It is useful to familiarise yourself (on the NSC website) with the various details for this wherever your geographical location. You may want to find what to expect in the area where you live and what will be happening where you are working in clinical practice. Make sure that you select the appropriate country. The UK National Screening Committee manages the specific programmes for cancer screening in the UK. It issues guidance on which screening programmes should be supported and also gives details on how to implement and monitor them (NSC UK, 2010).

Breast screening

Breast screening involves taking a mammogram of each breast (an X-ray of the carefully compressed breasts). Potential patients may have a variety of concerns, both personal and cultural, about breast screening, so it is important to inform them that the staff at NHS breast screening units in the UK are women only. If a patient worries that the procedure sounds painful, then reassure her that women who take up the screening test remark that is quite uncomfortable but not painful. This may make a difference as to whether a woman will attend her screening appointment. The mammogram can detect small changes in breast tissue, which may be too small to feel on breast examination, for either the woman or her practice nurse. The invitation to attend breast screening is given to women aged between the ages of 50 and 70, every three years (in Northern Ireland the upper age limit is 64). Women over the age of 70 are not sent invitations but are encouraged to make their own appointments. From 2012, it is planned that the screening programme will extend the age range to between 47 and 73 (DH, 2010b).

Women currently under the age of 50 with a family history of breast cancer will be offered regular screening and may also have the addition of a different type of screening test with an MRI scan (magnetic resonance imaging). This type of screening is found to be more sensitive for screening the dense breast tissue in the younger women (MARBIS, 2005). Research to support screening in younger women with relatives with breast cancer has added to the debate to extend the screening programme further, thereby preventing deaths from cancer, suggesting specifically yearly screening for women aged 40–49 (Kopans, 2010).

Encouraging women to be aware of their breasts, that is, to know what they look and feel like at different times, should assist women to understand what is normal for them and therefore detect any unusual changes. This approach is supported by the 'Be breast aware' leaflet produced by the NHS Breast Screening Programme and Cancer Research UK, published in 2006 and available in 19 languages. The Department of Health's policy on breast awareness, supported strongly by the nursing and medical profession, does not advocate routine self-examination to a set technique, but does encourage women to check their breasts and know what is normal for them, and therefore know when changes occur (DH, 2006b). The scientific evidence to support formal, ritual self-examination, performed at the same time each month, is lacking. Instead, the NHS screening programme sets out a five-point plan:

- know what is normal for you;
- look and feel;
- know what changes to look for;
- report changes without delay;
- attend breast screening if aged 50 and over.

It may be useful to be aware of the fact that some women in the UK will consult American websites about breast examination. They will find that the ritual of routine self-examination, to a set technique, at a set time each month, is still encouraged in that country. This may cause confusion, but careful direction to the NHS breast screening programme and the Cancer Research UK five-point plan should give clarification. You may wish to get your own copy of the five-point plan to familiarise yourself with the guidelines, so that you can have a well-informed discussion with any patient who may raise this issue.

Activity 3.1   *Communication*

A woman approaches you in clinic and asks for advice. She is puzzled about the breast-screening programme, as she has reached her 50th birthday and has not yet been sent her invitation to attend a screening unit for a mammogram. She is worried that she has been left out of the system.

- What response do you offer her?

There is an outline answer to this at the end of the chapter.

More people in the UK are aware of breast cancer in women, due to strong and repeated health promotion campaigns. People shopping in high street pharmacies or clothing stores will be familiar with breast aware month in October each year and will find pink ribbon lapel badges on sale, to raise funds for cancer research. Many people are unaware, however, of the fact that men can also develop breast cancer. Men have a small amount of breast tissue behind each nipple and it is here that the breast cancer can develop. Breast cancer in men is rare, and there is no screening programme. In the UK around 300 men are diagnosed each year and like women, the single biggest risk is age. Most cases are diagnosed between the ages of 60 and 70 years (Cancer Research UK, 2009).

Recently, within the UK there have been some awareness-raising campaigns for improving breast cancer screening programmes for black women. The argument is that for many years the 'face' for women's breast cancer has been the white middle-class woman, who features in posters and advertisements raising awareness. Lack of a wider range of ethnic images adds to the perception that other groups of women are not at such risk of developing breast cancer. This has led to women being diagnosed late, and inequalities in survival rates. Evidence for this has come from a small UK study (Bowen et al., 2008) with more studies carried out in the USA on African-American women. These studies demonstrated that black women develop breast cancer, on average, 10 to 20 years younger than white women. Black women were less at risk of developing breast cancer, but, for those that did, it had a tendency to be a more aggressive type of breast cancer. This has implications for the screening age set currently at 50 (to be changed to 47 from 2012), as this is too high a starting age for black women.

Case study: Learning disability and breast cancer screening

Fiona acts as carer for her sister, Rosie, who is aged 52 with learning disabilities. Fiona is concerned when a letter arrives inviting Rosie to attend a mammography appointment, as part of the local breast screening

continued overleaf...

continued...

programme. Fiona wonders how she should proceed with this appointment for Rosie, who lacks the mental capacity to make her own decisions about screening. Following consultation with Rosie's practice nurse she learns that she may make a 'best interest' decision. That is, she makes a decision on behalf of Rosie in the same way that she makes decisions about other aspects of Rosie's care and treatment. Whether a person is a paid carer, unpaid family member or close friend, the process is the same. The practice nurse tells Fiona of a publication about making best interest decisions that she feels will give her clear information (OPG, 2009). She also reminds Fiona that staff at the NHS mobile screening unit are all women (Rosie will find this acceptable) and that she can phone the radiographer in advance to let them know about Rosie. Together they agree that Rosie, if possible, should have the mammogram as their mother had breast cancer.

Cervical screening

Cervical screening is not a test for cancer. It is, however, a test (known as a smear test) which takes a sample of cells from a woman's cervix using a special brush; a practice nurse or doctor does this test. A cytologist carefully examines the sample. By detection of any abnormal cells and commencing early treatment, it prevents cancer of the cervix developing. Women in the age group 25 to 49 are invited every three years for cervical screening and those aged 50 to 64, every five years, in England. Cervical cancer is very rare in women under 25 (DH, 2010b). In Northern Ireland and Wales, the screening is offered to women between the ages of 20 and 64 and in Scotland from the ages of 20 to 60.

Activity 3.2   *Communication*

A family friend approaches you for advice, as she knows you are a nurse. She is 25 years old and has received a letter calling her for a cervical screening test (cervical smear), but she tells you that she has not been sexually active since she was at college. She thinks that she needn't bother with the test but wants to be sure that she is correct.

- What is your response?

There is an outline response at the end of this chapter.

Recent research (Gok et al., 2010) indicates that the availability of self-sampling test kits to detect the human papilloma virus (HPV) in women would increase screening availability. The HPV can cause damage to cervical cells and this may develop into cervical cancer. It is suggested that this method of collecting cervico-vaginal specimens is an effective way of increasing coverage in a screening programme. The NHS is piloting research for this testing as an 'add on' to traditional screening, as not all younger women take up the invitation for cervical smear testing. The researchers believe that this form of screening could double the number of women diagnosed with HPV, as women are more likely to carry out self-testing at home. Non-attendance to smear test screening, particularly among younger women, is a major concern in the effectiveness of current cervical screening programmes in the UK. The data suggests that one woman in five does not attend appointments sent out to them (Weller and Campbell, 2009). Any alterations to the current cervical screening programme would require rigorous testing and research to provide evidence before any changes could be implemented. (See Chapter 6 for HPV vaccines in 12–13-year-old girls in the UK).

Bowel cancer screening

Bowel cancer screening aims to detect cancer at early stages in symptom-free people, when treatment is likely to be effective. It can also detect polyps (tumours found on mucosal surfaces; they are usually benign but can develop into cancer in time). The removal of the polyp will reduce the risk of bowel cancer. Screening of people involves participants being sent a postal test kit. In their homes they can carry out three stool tests for faecal occult blood (FOB). They follow clear guidelines provided with an instruction sheet. The completed test kits are then posted to a regional laboratory for analysis. Any woman or man with a positive result will be invited for a colonoscopy (bowel scope) to see if polyps or cancer are present. In England and Wales women and men are eligible for this screening programme every two years, from the ages 60 to 69, and they are automatically sent the test kit in the post. People over 70 can request a screening kit. The screening service should be available to all people aged 70 to 74 years in England and in Wales by 2015 (DH, 2010b). In Scotland the age range for men and women is 50 to 74 years.

Activity 3.3   *Communication*

A neighbour approaches you, as she knows you are a nurse. She has found out that she is under the age set for bowel cancer screening, but she is worried as her sister had bowel cancer two years ago. She confides that she has symptoms of change in bowel habits and asks you if she should be asking to be screened.

- What is your response?

There is an outline response at the end of the chapter.

The government has announced recent additional developments in bowel cancer screening. Following a 16-year clinical trial, co-funded by Cancer Research, the funding has been secured for a four-year programme (Cancer Research UK, 2010). With UK National Screening Committee approval, the screening pilot tests commenced in 2011 with the expectation that a full programme will be commenced by 2016 in England and be available to men and women aged between 55 and 59. This new screening test involves using a flexible sigmoidoscope, known as the 'flexi-scope'. The flexi-scope is placed in the rectum and lower bowel, to facilitate an illuminated examination and removal of any small growths or polyps. Removal of these growths at an early stage can help prevent cancer developing later. The new programme is based on research conducted in 14 UK centres (Atkin et al., 2010). Nurses will have a special role in this new 'flexi-scope' screening programme. Training of nurse endoscopists already occurs in many centres and it would be expected that training opportunities would increase to meet clinical needs.

> ### Case study: Bowel cancer screening, the need to confirm understanding in those requiring assistance
>
> *Cynthia is a community nurse involved in the team of carers looking after 65-year-old Mrs B in her own home. Mrs B uses a wheelchair and requires assistance with hygiene needs. One morning Cynthia arrives to find that Mrs B has received a bowel screening kit in the post and she shows this to Cynthia. They look together at the instructions for sample collecting in the guidelines that accompany the test kit. Cynthia takes note of the fact that Mrs B has a good understanding of what the bowel screening is offering; she understands about the three stool samples for faecal occult blood (FOB). Further, Cynthia also takes note of the fact that Mrs B has a full understanding of what a colonoscopy examination entails. On the basis of this comprehensive understanding, when Mrs B asks Cynthia if she can have assistance in completing the tests in the kit, Cynthia agrees. She knows that Mrs B has the mental capacity to consent to the screening.*

Prostate cancer risk management programme (PCRMP)

Currently there is no national screening programme for prostate cancer (Burford et al., 2010). There is a commitment to the introduction of a future programme, however, if and when screening and treatment techniques are well developed. The PCRMP was introduced in England in 2009. Wales, Scotland and Northern Ireland have followed on with the programme and all areas distribute information packs to GPs. Men under the age of 50 are considered low risk, therefore the test is offered to men of 50 and over. Currently the PCRMP guidelines indicate that men considering being tested are given written information to explain about the test, followed by a consultation with the GP. They can then have a blood test to measure the PSA (prostate-specific antigen) level. The prostate gland is found only in men, below the bladder and surrounding the urethra.

> ### Activity 3 .4   *Communication*
>
> A gentleman approaches you in an outpatient's clinic and tells you that his wife has read in the newspaper about a special test for men to check for prostate cancer. He wonders if this is correct and if so, would it be appropriate for him have the test, as his father had prostate cancer.
>
> *There is an outline response at the end of this chapter.*

Uptake of UK screening services

Methods employed to encourage the uptake of screening services are thematised in the report by Cancer Research UK (2008). It is useful to consider these initiatives or actions, as this should increase your understanding of how and why NHS screening may or may not have a 'good' uptake where you live or where you work in clinical practice. The report lists seven initiatives or areas of good practice.

Research summary: Good practice in screening services (Cancer Research UK, 2008)

'Joint working'

The idea is to ensure that the same messages get put across about the screening programmes available and that best use is made of staff expertise and equipment. Joint working also includes awareness-raising campaigns, for example, to encourage the use of the screening services and remove barriers to understanding in certain population areas. The report identifies local community health organisations working along with other organisations. For example, this could be neighbouring community health organisations, hospital trusts, private and voluntary sectors.

'Public campaigns and health promotion'

The report gives examples of media campaigns to raise awareness, particularly targeting ethnic communities with low uptake.

'Targeting community initiatives'

This might be a specific geographical area that is a community or it might be a specific age group of people who would be focused upon for screening.

'Workings within GP practices'

The report highlights the usefulness of, for example, in-surgery poster displays and links with local pharmacies.

'Service improvements'

This means providing extra locations for screening facilities and extending the hours, sometimes giving a choice of attending different locations, again focusing on a particular target group.

'Equity audits and research'

This is about the gathering of information about certain groups in the population, to identify low uptake, to have future specific targeting and better understanding of uptake.

'Screening databases'

This is not a direct method of improving uptake of screening. However, improved, updated databases of current eligible individuals would have an impact on those populations offered screening coverage. This is particularly important in mobile populations.

The 'one size fits all' approach to health information is not appropriate in meeting the needs of the UK's increasingly diverse population and there is a constant need to find ways to target groups and communities that have a low uptake of screening services, in other words a variety of approaches. Health literacy (see Chapter 4) varies to a large extent in the population, and socio-economic status is a powerful driver of uptake of

continued opposite...

continued...

screening (Weller and Campbell, 2009). Within the UK there is a wide variation in uptake in cancer screening programmes among different populations or groups of people (health inequalities in Chapter 6).

To see how nurses might go about the business of behaviour change in relation to uptake of health screening, refer back to behaviour change methods in Chapter 2.

The following screening programmes are not all about cancer prevention. The screening is still about actions to improve health, to test for hidden disease, or disease at an early stage.

Diabetic retinopathy screening

The National Service Framework (NSF) for diabetes has two parts: firstly a set of national standards (DH, 2001) to improve health outcomes for people with diabetes; and secondly, a delivery strategy (DH, 2003a), which sets out national targets for NHS performance towards the standards. This includes routine screening for diabetic retinopathy (vascular changes in the retinal blood vessels), a visual impairment which can result from having diabetes. The aim of the screening programme is to reduce the risk of sight loss, by prompt identification and effective treatment of sight-threatening retinopathy at appropriate stages during the disease process. The screening test involves taking a photograph of the retina (back of the eye) in each eye, by digital photography. By using a grading process of the photographic results, the eyes can be screened for signs of retinopathy. The target aims to cover 100% of the population of people with diabetes (12 years of age and over) with annual screening. The minimum national standard is 80% of patients screened.

The health check (vascular risk)

This NHS health check programme for vascular risk started in April 2009 and it targets everyone between the ages of 40 and 74 to prevent heart disease, stroke, diabetes and kidney disease. All people not already diagnosed with one of these conditions will be invited every five years to have a check to assess their risk and receive advice and support to help reduce or manage any risk. It is planned that this will be a phased programme, expecting full programme implementation by 2012–13 (DH, 2009a) and that this will be carried out at GP practices. Some of this vascular health check will involve practice nurses.

Health screening for over 65s in the NHS

Some additional opportunities for health screening occurs for people in the older age group, while there is a continuation of screening started in earlier adulthood. As people get older they are more likely to develop conditions that are rare in younger people. Men and women over 65 continue to be invited to bowel cancer screening until the age of 70 years. There are now plans to extend this age range further (see above). Over this age, people can continue to have screening by request. Breast cancer screening for women will continue up to age 70, with plans to extend this to 73 (see above). Requests by individuals can be made to local screening units to be included in the screening beyond this age. Women from the age of 65 no longer receive an invitation for cervical screening, unless they have had a previous abnormal screening result from any of the past three screening tests. Women who have never undertaken screening are entitled to ask for a test, regardless of age.

AAA screening

The NHS abdominal aortic aneurysm (AAA) programme was introduced nationwide in England from the spring of 2009 (in Scotland from 2011). This programme is for men when they reach the age of 65 (over 65s may request this screening), who are offered an invitation to screening to measure the width of the aorta, involving a simple ultrasound scan of the abdomen. The aorta is the main blood vessel supplying blood to the body. In some people, the wall of the aorta can, with age, become weak and start to swell, forming an aneurysm. The aim of this screening is to reduce the number of deaths related to this condition, most common in men aged 65 and over. Wales and Northern Ireland have still to set deadlines for commencement of screening, in line with the advice from the National Screening Committee (NHS, 2011).

Opportunistic screening

Screening can be considered to be opportunistic when a test is carried out for a patient, during a consultation for a completely different condition. The appointment has given an excellent opportunity to discuss other relevant health matters.

Scenario: An example of opportunistic screening

A middle-aged man comes to the general practice where you are on placement. He has backache. The records state that he last attended the practice five years ago. Following the back pain consultation, the GP refers him straight away to the practice nurse for blood pressure testing. The practice nurse is coordinating vascular risk screening in the practice. Here is a chance to obtain a measurement of his blood pressure. The only way of knowing if an individual has high blood pressure is to have it measured. Many people who have high blood pressure have no symptoms at all; as a result it can often go undiagnosed (British Heart Foundation, 2009). One in every three adults and just over three in ten men have high blood pressure.

The national chlamydia screening programme (NCSP)

The NCSP in England was established in 2003, to offer free opportunistic screening, treatments, partner management and prevention, to sexually active men and women under the age of 25. The goals of the programme are to prevent and control chlamydia through early detection and treatment of asymptomatic infection, reduce the transmission of infection to sexual partners and prevent the consequences of untreated infection. The white paper, Our Health, Our Care, Our Say (DH, 2006a) presented a new direction for community services, identifying a need to improve sexual health provision as a key priority for primary care. Nationally, the most commonly diagnosed bacterial sexually transmitted infection is chlamydia, with the highest rate in the 16 to 24 age group. Untreated, it can have serious consequences. Women can develop pelvic inflammatory disease (PID), ectopic pregnancy and tubal infertility. Men can develop epididymitis and epididymo-orchitis. The commitment from the coalition government to keep up with chlamydia screening in England continues and is outlined in the white paper, Healthy Lives, Healthy People (DH, 2010a).

Community nurses can have a particular role in chlamydia screening, working in GP practice. Also, chlamydia screening teams (nurses) based in the community conduct outreach projects which target young people. Health education events such as health fairs are often held in colleges and universities. Nurses raise awareness about chlamydia, offering and encouraging participants to take up screening and giving out test kits, which can then be completed in privacy by the young person. The test kit comprises either a urine test for men or a vaginal swab (like a tampon) for women. After the test is completed the kit can be either posted to the testing laboratory direct or handed back to the community nurse, who then forwards all kits for analysis. The participant is then contacted with the result and if positive then they will be prescribed a course of antibiotics.

Screening new patients at GP practices

As well as the screening programmes mentioned above there are many tests that people may expect to be carried out by their GP and they include the 'new patient health check', where selected tests are carried out as part of this routine screening. This involves measuring height and weight, checking up on current vaccination status, general health, diet and physical activity advice, urinalysis testing and blood pressure testing. The British Hypertension Society advises that all adults have a blood pressure check every five years, or every year if they are over 75 or if they have high blood pressure (Williams et al., 2004).

Occupational health screening

Occupational health is concerned with the health and welfare of people engaged in work or employment. It actively promotes the maintenance of good health in the workplace and supports employers and employees when health problems occur. The aim of screening in occupational health is to advise managers on the prospective employees' fitness for the job requirements. This advice would be where necessary, on any adjustments to work content or environment that might be needed, in view of any disability in line with the Equality Act of 2010; to identify any work-related health risks of future employment. A health screening programme will help detect disease or risk factors early so that further progression can be stopped or the outcome improved. The three elements to the screening are as follows:

- To complete a full health questionnaire: there may be a consultation with the prospective employee's GP. Occupational health screening may stop at this point if all is satisfactory.
- Further assessment, if necessary, following completion of the questionnaire will involve offering a clinic appointment with the occupational health service department, to ascertain fitness to work.
- Immunisation where recommended, at the beginning of employment, will be arranged by and administered by the occupational health services.

At this point you may think back to the occupational health screening that you undertook as you commenced your own nursing education programme. You will probably now understand better the process of assessment of your fitness for practice in the clinical settings, and the risk detection offered by screening.

The future for screening services: nurses in the high street

Recent pilot studies have commenced in a leading UK pharmacy where nurse-led clinics are available. Nurses can offer mole screening, travel vaccinations, osteoporosis risk assessments and a healthy heart screening. The heart screening includes calculating body mass index (BMI), blood pressure, cholesterol and blood glucose testing. Nurses can provide lifestyle advice (see Chapter 2) and if needed, refer customers to their GP. This move is in line with current coalition government policy to improve access to health services at convenient times. Patients will pay for services initially, but future bids for NHS contracts by pharmacy chains could be providing a mixture of free and paid-for services to patients across the country (Wallis, 2010).

Case study: A future nurse in a pharmacy

A 22-year-old woman speaks to the pharmacy nurse, requesting emergency hormonal contraception (the morning-after pill). The customer is told that she needs to consult the pharmacist (who has been specially trained to prescribe this). As part of the private consultation with the nurse, the nurse suggests a chlamydia screening test (opportunistic screening). As a result of unprotected sex, there may be a possible high risk of exposure to chlamydia for this young woman.

Chapter summary

This chapter has raised your awareness of large scale national screening programmes available in the UK and their contribution to health and wellbeing for patients. It has outlined the range of screening that individuals could expect to experience during their lifespan. Patients often turn to their nurse for clarification and explanation of matters relating to health, therefore it is important that nurses are well informed about the role of health promotion and raising awareness about screening. Nurses can encourage and support patients as they take up invitations to partake in screening, which has the potential to save lives or improve quality of life. Health promotion must have an advocacy function, which includes the encouragement of informed debate and discussion, as new evidence and policy emerges for extended or new large scale screening programmes. Nurses need to be aware of this.

Activities: Brief outline answers

Activity 3.1 (page 46)

You can begin your reply to this woman by explaining that the NHS screening programme is a rolling programme, that is, a system that will call women from their GP's practices in turn. This will mean that not all women are sent their invitation to attend as soon as they have their 50th birthday. The invitation will arrive some time between the ages of 50 and 53 and the women will automatically be sent this if they are registered with a GP.

It is good advice to ensure that patients keep their GP practice up to date with correct contact details. You can reassure the woman by informing her that she could get in touch with her practice and ask to speak to the practice nurse. She can then ask where the practice is on the schedule for their screening to be carried out and so calculate roughly when she is likely to be sent her invitation.

Activity 3.2 (page 47)

You should explain the facts to your family friend so that she can make her decision about her health screening. There is evidence to show that if a woman has never been sexually active then her risk of developing cervical cancer is extremely low. The language used here is not 'no risk' but 'low risk'.

If a woman has ever had sex she will probably have come into contact with the human papilloma virus (HPV), which causes cervical cancer. The evidence suggests, therefore, that it is appropriate to accept the appointment and have the cervical smear test. She may like to contact her practice nurse, who will carry out the test and explain to her what is exactly involved.

Activity 3.3 (page 48)

Your response must be that it is unwise for your neighbour to wait for screening in this instance. Persistent change in bowel habits or anxiety about bowel health in general should be investigated. Your neighbour must be encouraged to seek medical advice urgently and consult her GP, who could arrange for referral to a specialist if necessary, in view of her family history.

Activity 3.4 (page 49)

Your reply should confirm with this man that his wife would have read about the prostate testing offered to men aged 50 and over.

Are some men more at risk of developing prostate cancer? The biggest risk factor is age and other factors include men with a family history. In the UK risk is also greater in black Caribbean and black African men. His question about his father could be significant, especially if this prostate cancer occurred before the age of 60.

It is important that men receive the best available information and support. This man needs to be given a written information sheet from his practice, which fully explains what is involved in the test. He will also need to have a consultation with his GP. If he goes ahead with the test he will need to understand that this will involve having a blood test. The PSA (prostate-specific antigen) levels in the blood are measured. This substance, made by the prostate gland, naturally leaks into the bloodstream. A raised level can be an early indication of prostate cancer. However, prostatitis, enlargement of the prostate and urinary infection can also cause a rise in PSA.

Useful websites

www.cancerscreening.nhs.uk/breastscreen/breastawareness.html
Useful site with breast awareness leaflet.

www.cancerresearchuk.org
A wide range of information about cancer screening, cancer treatments and campaigns.

www.cancerhelp.org.uk/type/prostate-cancer/about/screening-for-prostate-cancer
Cancer research UK facts on prostate screening.

Chapter 4
Teaching patients

NMC Standards for Pre-registration Nursing Education

This chapter will address the following competencies:

Domain 2: Communication and interpersonal skills

2. All nurses must use a range of communication skills and technologies to support person-centred care and enhance quality and safety. They must ensure people receive all the information they need in a language and manner that allows them to make informed choices and share decision-making. They must recognise when language interpretation or other communication support is needed and know how to obtain it.
3. All nurses must use the full range of communication methods, including verbal, non-verbal and written, to acquire, interpret and record their knowledge and understanding of people's needs. They must take account of the many different ways in which people communicate and how these may be influenced by ill health, disability and other factors and be able to recognise and respond effectively when a person finds it hard to communicate.

NMC Essential Skills Clusters

This chapter will address the following ESCs:

Cluster: Care, compassion and communication

6. People can trust the newly registered graduate nurse to engage therapeutically and actively listen to their needs and concerns, responding using skills that are helpful, providing information that is clear, accurate, meaningful and free from jargon.

By the first progression point:

1. Communicates effectively both orally and in writing, so that the meaning is always clear.
3. Always seeks to confirm understanding.

By entry to the register:

8. Communicates effectively and sensitively in different settings, using a range of methods and skills.
11. Is proactive and creative in enhancing communication and understanding.

Introduction

Case study: A poor teaching environment

Mr Patel attends an appointment for a teaching session about his new dietary restrictions, following his recently diagnosed coronary heart disease. The appointment has been arranged with staff nurse Brown in the cardiology outpatients' department. The department is busy and the nurse puts two chairs together around a table in the corner of the big waiting room. The nurse assumes that he must need to understand why a restriction must be made on the level of fats in his diet because of what happens to the body when there is this excess. She begins her teaching sessions by spreading out many leaflets on the table.

Mr Patel, however, wants to know about the following things: he does not know how long the appointment is expected to last, he wants to know what the word 'restrictions' means exactly, and he wonders if this will mean he has to miss out some of his favourite foods. He thinks that this may last for a few weeks as he vaguely remembers hearing a programme on the radio about dieting. He wonders how he is ever going to explain this 'restriction' to his wife, who does all the cooking. He also is reluctant to tell the pleasant nurse that he doesn't understand the terminology she is using.

He glances anxiously at the many leaflets, noticing that they are small print (he has forgotten his reading glasses).

Nurses are expected to engage in good communication skills and whether working in hospital or community settings, all nurses have the responsibility of carrying out health teaching with their patients. This role has to be considered carefully, providing information that is clear, accurate and meaningful. This will mean that nurses must engage with the various elements and aspects of being an approachable and effective teacher of health.

Staff nurse Brown in the case study above has made assumptions about what Mr Patel needs or wants to know. She has not prepared a good environment or plan for his teaching. This chapter will consider what it means to be a good teacher of health and understand why and how staff nurse Brown went wrong. It will look first at where teaching should be carried out, and then look at how people learn, considering barriers to learning. The chapter also helps you to think about how to plan learning, what methods you might use to teach and finally how to evaluate your teaching.

Where to carry out teaching

Nurses need to think carefully about where their teaching time with patients will be spent. The setting might be general practice, outpatient clinics, hospital or the patient's home. Finding a suitable location within the setting is important. Planning ahead if possible for privacy and uninterrupted time must be given particular thought, and the possible inclusion of partners, husbands, wives, a parent or carers as part of the teaching session, if appropriate. Alongside the careful choice of space and surroundings within the setting, to carry out teaching nurses must consider the level of motivation that their patients may or may not have. The role of the nurse in carrying out teaching is therefore to be as practical and realistic as possible and to recognise the circumstances and need of each individual patient. There is a need to plan your teaching to take into account the distinctive requirements of the patients. For example, some patients may find it difficult to say what it is they want to learn in terms of understanding what they need to know about their health. The reasons for this might be embarrassment, lack of familiarity with medical or technical terminology, denial of illness, pain, or a disempowering feeling that the professionals know best.

How to carry out teaching and readiness to learn

When talking to people about health matters, nurses need to avoid using jargon or technical language, which may confuse or alienate. By introducing some structure to the teaching, patients will be able to absorb the information and nurses can facilitate deep learning (understanding) as opposed to just memorising (surface learning). By this we mean that nurses need to find out what patients already know and understand and then proceed from this point. The next step would be to clarify and explain any unknown technical terms. This should help with future communications and could be useful when patients have discussions with other healthcare professionals. This structured approach to teaching should help start a partnership in communication. Additional points to consider are that there may be a limit to patients' memory capacity. Dividing the information into small amounts for teaching on more than one session may be useful, rather than packing all the information into one long session.

Barriers to learning

Patients are not always ready to learn, or indeed willing to learn. Judging a patient's ability to absorb your teaching is an important first step. Your aim may be to empower the patient by giving them all the information they need as you feel this is so vital. However, you must first think what could cause barriers to this process.

Think back to an occasion in which you observed a patient being taught. Did you notice that they were not listening, or saying they had had enough? Consider what was going on for that patient at the time.

- Could there have been internal physical barriers such as pain or tiredness?
- Could there have been internal emotional barriers such as distress, fear or depression?
- Perhaps the patient was unable to understand because they did not have the intellectual capacity – too young, poor memory, not well educated.
- Was there anything in the external environment interfering with learning, such as noise, distractions, cold?
- Could it be the content of the session or the way the nurse taught, such as too much jargon, too fast, not well explained? Perhaps the nurse did not look interested, or did not understand the topic herself.

Further guidance on this activity is given at the end of the chapter.

Having looked at possible barriers to learning, you can now appreciate more how complex teaching patients can be. Patients are not always in a position to receive nurses' carefully planned teaching. On the other hand, you will meet patients eager and ready to learn, sometimes asking you questions before you are prepared.

How people learn

People tend to learn in similar ways when ready. You will remember learning new things yourself; how you struggled with new terminology and perhaps took time to grasp why there are several ways of thinking and doing in nursing, when you couldn't see the difference as yet. A theory of learning which may help you think of levels of learning is that of Bloom (1984).

Concept summary: Bloom (1984)

Bloom's taxonomy (or levels) of learning explains how people build up from basic knowledge to being able to use that knowledge to make judgements about the topic – to 'know' it so well that they can decide on its worth.

- Knowledge: recalling and remembering information, facts and principles. What is it?
- Comprehension: understanding and interpreting that knowledge, without seeing the implications yet. What does it mean?
- Application: seeing the use for something, how it fits in with a theory or practice in real life. How do I use it?
- Analysis: breaking down into parts, recognising connections and differences. What does it consist of?
- Synthesis: putting things together to make a whole in a new way of thinking. Making a proposal or a plan. How does it come together as a whole?

continued opposite...

continued...

- Evaluation: making judgements about the values of things. Measuring them against criteria of appraisal. Is it a good thing?

You can use these levels to decide how much you want the patient to learn and how much you can teach them at any one time, for example in a series of sessions. It is probably enough in the first short session for the patient to know and understand their new diagnosis. Having reflected on that level, next time you could discuss how it will affect their daily life and later, what choices the patient has in the management of their diagnosis.

Scenario

Mrs Carter is about to have a hysterectomy and firstly needs to learn the medical terminology (knowledge) so that the word being used becomes familiar to her. She then needs to understand (comprehension) what this means, perhaps in terms of 'removal of my womb'. Ask her to explain it to you. Thinking what this means for her (application), she needs to know that this will stop her menstruation.

Bloom's three higher levels of learning go further, although Mrs Carter says to the nurse teaching her, 'that's all I need to know thank you'. You could perhaps leave the rest for another time.

Next day she asks the nurse to explain how the surgery will be done – will she have stitches, and where, and what exactly will be removed? She's thinking of the details (analysis). Following this level of learning a person gains insight into the 'whole' idea (synthesis) and Mrs Carter realises that this will be major surgery. She will need to be in hospital for a while, and she will need to rest and not take strenuous exercise for a few weeks. She begins to ask when she can go home and manage her toddler son. Until now she has not thought to ask if she will go through the menopause. Finally an overall appraisal of the interruption to her life is possible (evaluation) now she is 'qualified' to make an informed choice to go ahead and she has the in-depth learning to make a plan for the future, free from the influence of fear of the unknown, or persuasion from others.

Recognise that this theory also applies to you learning nursing, while you are reading this – it applies to your learning how to teach patients.

Planning teaching

Consider how often you have sat in teaching sessions and thought it was becoming hard to concentrate for that length of time. You are well and ready to learn. A patient may be able to concentrate only for a much shorter time. Five or ten minutes is often enough time for a patient teaching session. Twenty minutes for a one-to-one session would be the maximum.

Teaching should, of course, begin when the patient is ready and asking questions, or you may see that they are getting better and need to know more well before they go home. Do not think it has to be done all at once, and certainly well before they go home.

....

Case study: Planned teaching sessions

Steven Walker is a lead nurse in an acute coronary care unit. The unit has high and medium dependency areas and Steven would like to organise patient teaching for patients who have had a myocardial infarction (heart attack).

He knows that some information is better given earlier if the patient is anxious to know what has happened and what is happening now, but not all the information can be given at once. He makes a plan of sessions to be delivered during every patient's average seven day stay in the unit. The plan can of course be modified as appropriate.

Having made his plan, Steven then set about making each session much more detailed with ideas for the information required.

....

It is a good idea to have some general teaching plans to be used for groups of similar patients like this. It incorporates nursing knowledge of what the patients need to know, and how much they can learn while in hospital in this case. Community nurses could use the same principle to design teaching plans for use in patients' homes. Each patient is different of course and the plan will have to be modified as it is implemented in practice. Some suggested modifications can be incorporated in the details, as Steven has done for men, women and elderly patients.

Detailed teaching materials need to be prepared by each clinical area and kept in a folder for use by nurses teaching the sessions. Steven has made a collection including a model and diagram of a heart, some printed material on healthy eating, explanations of the common drugs used, leaflets explaining the rehabilitation classes, and leaflets from the British Heart Foundation. Nurses using the teaching folder make sure that the material is up to date. In addition the unit computer should be used to access information.

When using any teaching plan for a patient, whether pre-prepared or designed with the individual in mind, it is essential to begin with asking what the patient knows already. A good start to a teaching session would be to ask the patient what they know about the topic of the session. You then know what to go over as a reminder, and what is new information for the patient.

Activity 4.2   *Communication*

Outline teaching plans for one of the following patients. Consider the variation in learning ability between them. Suggest some teaching resources to use.

- A child of 10 who needs to learn how to understand and use an inhaler when he/she has a asthma attack
- A 28-year-old woman with a learning disability who was seen in casualty having poked a metal hair grip into her outer ear to clear wax. She has a superficial infection.
- An elderly woman with depression and self-neglect who needs to manage a course of oral antibiotics.
- A 45-year-old man who has been diagnosed with non-insulin-dependent diabetes and says he doesn't understand why people are concerned about his feet.

There is an outline answer for this activity at the end of the chapter.

You will have noticed some of the variables in learning ability in the patients from the last activity. Age and mental ability alter the level of learning which can be achieved, but nurses can address this through adapting their teaching to suit the patient's level. Guidance on teaching children, people with learning disabilities and altered mental states is not possible in detail here and we suggest you look at specialised books and relevant organisations for more information.

Teaching a skill

Some of your teaching will be about helping patients to acquire skills as well as knowledge. The activity above has the examples of using an inhaler and cleaning ears. You will meet patients who need to learn how to use equipment such as syringes and blood sugar monitors. Some patients need to know and how to undertake procedures such as self-catheterisation and managing a feeding tube. Most of what the patient needs to know is what *you* have learned about the skill, with adaptations for using the equipment at home, not in hospital.

Activity 4.3   *Reflection*

Think of a single skill (practical procedure) you have acquired – a procedure or how to use a piece of equipment.

- How did you learn that skill? Recall methods of teaching that you were exposed to.
- How did these methods help you learn? Did you then learn further by yourself – how?
- How do you know you have acquired the skill?

There is an outline answer for this activity at the end of the chapter.

Having thought about planning teaching for individual patients in some detail, we now come to some specific ideas for teaching before going on to evaluating patient teaching.

Group teaching

Quite often, teaching in a small group can be a most effective method to facilitate learning in health promotion. People can join in with discussion and share experiences and they can ask questions of each other. By accepting an invitation to attend the group teaching session, patients and their relatives are making a commitment, and this may have a positive effect on learning because they feel that others are in the same situation.

Activity 4.4   *Communication*

You are currently on placement in the community. A group of five women currently take medication for high blood pressure. They have individually attended appointments with the practice nurse for blood pressure monitoring and general health advice related to their blood pressure levels. There is a new approach for teaching patients at the GP practice. These women have been especially invited together to attend a group teaching session

continued overleaf...

: *continued...*

about weight loss. The practice nurse suggests that you run the new teaching session with her support.

- How do you go about this?

There is an outline answer for this activity at the end of the chapter.

Whether teaching groups or individuals, at some stage you will be using printed information materials, usually leaflets, although information sheets and cards are commonly used for short instructions. There are many of these available from government or other national organisations and charities. You may be writing them yourself for your patient care areas.

Written information

A frequently used aid to teaching or information giving is in the use of information sheets, or what's often called 'patient information leaflets' (PILs) (Iddo and Prigat, 2004). Health professionals widely use them when involved in patient education or health promotion work.

Key issues of readability and legibility need to be considered when writing health information literature. Readability promotes meaning and understanding and depends on the choice of words and sentence length. Clarity of print and size of lettering aid the recognition and legibility of the words. The basic formula for a printed leaflet comprises: thinking of the words, deciding how many pictures and diagrams would be relevant and selecting the size of typeface and the layout. When writing for such materials, keep to clear, simple messages (DH, 2003b). Keep the intended reader focused in your mind while writing, avoid the use of jargon and define any technical words when they need to be introduced. Keep the use of acronyms to a minimum. Use short words and possibly consider the use of lists or bullet points to emphasise important issues. It is a good idea to pre-test the written material by giving it to someone to check that they can read it and understand it.

Concept summary: Written materials top tips

- Keep simply to one subject in each leaflet.
- Keep it up to date.
- Use everyday language and explain any medical terms used.
- Write directly and inclusively – using 'you' and 'we'.
- Use present and active tense i.e. 'your appointment is on ...' rather than 'an appointment has been made for...'.
- Write in short sentences.
- Give reasons for any instructions.
- Make the leaflet look interesting – with small blocks of text, bullet points, questions and answers – and leave some 'white' space in between writing.
- Use a plain (e.g. Arial) and large enough (at least 12 or 14 point) font.
- Limit the use of bold and other decorative ways of presentation.
- Use clear illustrations rather than representational images which do not show the real thing.

More guidelines are available from DH 2003b, RNIB 2004, MENCAP 2008, NHS 2010.

You may also find these tips useful in deciding which leaflets to stock in the clinical area. You may notice that some are not popular with patients because they are less easy to read or perhaps contain information which is too complicated.

Nurses teaching their patients on a one-to-one basis can make best use of leaflets, by discussing them *with* the patient, pointing out the key sections that support the message they want to get across. It might be helpful to write in the margins or circle a paragraph or diagram, to reinforce or to emphasise and personalise the message as part of the discussion. Other methods of using leaflets might be to leave them clearly displayed in an open area, the GP practice or hospital clinic for example. Organising an attractive, tidy display of the leaflets is a useful technique. People can look at them and quietly select them for reading if they are too embarrassed to ask for information. They can then read through the leaflet at their own pace and perhaps later, take any questions or points of discussion they may have to their healthcare professional.

A benefit of written information can be that patients can refer back to the material as required. There is less of a need for patients to take notes and it can reduce anxiety levels. It can be easy and cheap to produce basic written information. Mass produced leaflets, however, are not tailored to everyone's needs and they may contain advertising. In such instances nurses must be discerning and select appropriate leaflets for their teaching sessions. Will the leaflet be easily understood? Is it written in plain language? Is it available in other languages? Is it available in large print for visually impaired patients? Will it empower the patients? Will it encourage them to ask questions or discuss their health situation? It has to be remembered that any leaflet should be used alongside a face-to-face discussion and not used as a substitute for the health promoter.

Activity 4.5   *Communication*

You are currently on placement in a district general hospital in the outpatients' department. Your mentor asks if you would organise a display of patient information leaflets in one of the clinics by the end of the week. New display equipment has arrived in the department and has been unpacked ready for use. The old leaflets have been removed to a storeroom and the boxes of new leaflets are in Sister's office.

• How would you go about this?

There is an outline answer for this activity at the end of the chapter

Leaflets are not the only source of written material; these days more and more people are looking to the internet for health information.

Electronic media

Nurses need to be aware that many of the patients they spend time with may have accessed the internet to discover more about their health or their illness. The Office for National Statistics reported that 60% of adults in the UK access the internet almost every day. This means that 30.1 million adults are accessing the internet, double the estimate of 16.5 million in 2006 (Office for National Statistics, 2010). This evolution in information technology is bringing huge benefits to health promotion, enabling a seeking out of information and giving access to health information. Such health information is at the fingertips of people in their homes without having to access healthcare professionals and many websites provide helpful information for health promotion. There are challenges, however; not all the popular websites for health provide accurate and quality information. Any person can set up a website and some of that information may be incorrect. It is useful to check out information on health websites to ensure that you can suggest reliable sources of information to patients. For example, if authoritative sites, such as the Department of Health or the WHO give a link to the sites, it is likely to be genuine.

Hardyman et al. (2005) report that the internet on its own would be unlikely to replace person-to-person advice and support. Twenty-three per cent, almost a quarter, of the callers to a helpline for a cancer charity had already looked at the website before calling. The researchers found that the website would not totally replace the telephone helpline, that there was a need to talk to a person and that a mixture of both resources was needed (Hardyman et al 2005).

Whichever way, and with whatever resources you decide to teach patients, you will need to measure whether the teaching has been effective.

Evaluating teaching

There are two issues in evaluation of any teaching:

* what has been learned; the level of learning achieved;
* the quality of the teaching itself.

Learning can be evaluated through 'testing', as you know from your own learning of nursing. How you test patients may depend on their age, readiness and ability to learn as well as the content of the teaching plan. Knowledge can be tested by asking the patient to repeat the material back to you, or by giving a series of questions to answer. Some people (and often children) respond well to a quiz approach, perhaps with rewards in the form of praise or prizes. Group learning could be evaluated with a competition style of quiz, like a pub quiz. A skill can be tested by asking the patient to demonstrate it back to you.

In any situation if a patient has not remembered accurately or fully, then the teacher must accept this and give praise for trying and for what has been remembered. The material still to be learned, then needs to be repeated, without blame. Positive praise enhances learning; focusing on the negative does not.

Evaluating your own teaching can be done through reflection yourself, or by asking someone else to observe you and give you feedback. In addition, ask the patient to tell you what they think about your teaching. Issues to consider include:

* up-to-date material and resources;
* accuracy and whether everything important has been included;
* appropriate level (using Bloom);
* environment conducive to learning;
* appropriate timing and speed;

- quality (see top tips, page 64) of written resources;
- encouraging the patient to interact and ask questions;
- confident manner;
- recording of teaching in the patient's records.

Patient teaching is part of nursing care

It can be difficult to set aside time for teaching patients but it is essential for the patients' management of their own health (see Chapter 5). It also makes nursing care so much easier when the patients are well informed.

Learning needs can be assessed and recorded at the same time as other care needs. Just asking the patient why they are in the hospital, clinic or GP practice reveals a great deal about learning needs. Recording the patient's own words can help nurses planning the teaching understand what it is the patient knows.

As we have discussed, making general teaching plans for groups of patients can save time in gathering information and resources. Having a good supply of written materials on display will allow patients to read first and think of questions to ask.

Making time to teach every patient needs a confident and determined approach. You could begin by thinking that every patient will need some teaching input at admission, and then at intervals until prior to discharge. This will correct a common practice of only thinking of what the patient needs to know in terms of going home. Similarly checking on learning and teaching a little more often, each day or at each clinic or home visit perhaps, can become a part of your regular practice. Chapter 7 will go further to explore the relevant management elements of embedding health teaching into nursing practice.

Finally, the teaching and learning must be recorded in the patients' records. You could record every teaching session or even brief opportunities to give information in your daily reporting and recording. Steven in the coronary care unit has produced a single sheet summary of the teaching plan he devised. A copy of this sheet is amended by the nurse teaching a patient and then inserted into the patient's notes. The nurse writes the name of the patient, the dates of teaching and signs the record.

Before we leave this chapter, we want to introduce a broader view of the patient as a member of the community as well as someone under our care. Health information is relevant to all people and in a similar way to other skills for life such as IT skills, the skills of working with health information are increasingly useful to consumers of health.

Health literacy

The term health literacy has been used in the literature for many years. Individuals with undeveloped skills in reading and writing will not only have less exposure to traditional health education, but also less developed skills to act upon the information received. The Department of

Health states that health literacy is the relationship between a person's language and numeracy levels and their ability to receive, understand and process health information. Low levels of health literacy impact negatively on an individual's ability to take up action to improve their health (DH, 2007). Nurses need to consider therefore that health literacy depends on the level of literacy, language and numeracy skills that their patients may have. This in turn will impact on the ability of the patients to make informed health and lifestyle choices and also to 'navigate' an increasingly complex healthcare system. The WHO points out that health literacy means much more than the ability to read a leaflet and making health appointments. It is about the cognitive and social skills involved in being a patient. The degree of health literacy will determine the ability and motivation of individuals to access and understand and use effectively the heath information in ways that will promote good health. They see health literacy as essential to empowerment (WHO, 2009).

Chapter summary

This chapter has enabled you to explore and develop an understanding of some aspects of teaching patients. The chapter has focused on the organisation of teaching, which can be adapted for any care area. The ideas of readiness to learn and barriers to learning have been explored and written health materials have been examined. You need to have knowledge and comprehension of teaching and learning, follow the application to patients, analyse the components parts of the process and evaluate the importance of patient teaching to nursing care.

Activities: Brief outline answers

Activity 4.1 (page 60)

You could use a method of analysis for this activity:

- list the barriers you observed;
- for each one, describe the reasons you think they occurred – how did the nurse let them happen?
- give some ideas for removing or mediating these barriers – what could the nurse have done?
- consider how you could learn from this for your future practice.

Activity 4.2 (page 62)

The child of 10 with asthma is able at that age to understand, apply and even analyse information. He will be curious and questioning, perhaps showing off that he knows quite a lot already. On the negative side he may act resentfully and stubbornly refuse to cooperate. He needs to know:

- when to use the inhaler;
- how to breathe in the dose most effectively;
- what the drug does;
- how to store and clean the inhaler, and how to store the drug;
- to carry it all around safely and ready to use;
- to tell the teacher or a responsible person, such as the swimming pool attendant, that he may need to use it.

Resources you could use – the inhaler, the drug container and the instruction leaflets that come with them, model of the airways, leaflet from Asthma UK.

The woman with a learning disability is less likely to learn quickly and may only achieve a lower level of Bloom's taxonomy. She would learn better through real equipment and actual demonstration than through play acting or cartoon characters as she does not transfer the learning very well. She needs to know:

- what the outer ear looks like;
- that earwax is normal and needed to keep the dust out;
- not to put anything into her ear;
- to wash her ears with a finger and a clean flannel;
- to tell her carer if her ears are itchy or she can't hear well;
- how to use the cream prescribed for her infection.

Resources you could use – your ear to look at, some examples of bad things to use (cotton buds, hair clips) and let her see you throw them out, flannel over your finger to show how she must not go deeper into the ear, the cream so that she can see the right amount to use. Get her to use the correct method of washing.

The elderly woman's depression indicates that she is temporarily unable to learn very much, so you are going to have to instruct her with do's and don'ts rather than try to get her to understand and analyse. She needs to know:

- do take the tablets at regular intervals;
- do not miss any out;
- do finish the course;
- don't drink any alcohol until the course is finished;
- do tell the doctor or nurse if she feels sick or develops a rash.

Resources you could use – the packet of tablets and the leaflet that comes with it, a list of do's and don'ts to take away.

The 45-year-old diabetic man seems to be a capable adult learner so he should respond well to your teaching. However, he has a lack of understanding of his condition even though he has been taught previously. He may take some persuading to learn more since he thought he knew enough and now there is more for him to understand. He needs to know:

- that high blood sugar (when diabetes is not controlled well) means there is sugar in the tissues;
- that sugar in the tissues tends to encourage bacterial growth;
- that when tissue is damaged, for example blister and cuts on the feet, infection can get in and increase;
- that this means he must look after his vulnerable feet – keep them clean and free from damage;
- that he may need to consider new, better-fitting shoes;
- that he has access to a chiropodist, even just to have his toenails cut.

Resources you could use – model or diagram of a foot showing points of potential damage, photographs of problems with feet (infections, gangrene), leaflet from Diabetes UK, their website.

Activity 4.3 (page 63)

You may have been taught the skill by any of these methods of teaching:

- demonstration;
- supervised practice with patients;
- using models and simulated situations.

You may have learned further on your own by:

- continuing to practise handling the equipment without a patient;
- asking your mentor for opportunities to practice;
- reading more around the issue, to understand the rationale.

How do you know you have acquired the skill?

- you feel confident;
- you can do it without errors;
- you need less supervision;
- you can do it in reasonable and appropriate speed;
- you can teach someone else.

The same applies to the patients you teach.

Activity 4.4 (page 64)

- Establish how much time there is for your teaching session. Ask if this is one of other sessions or the only one?
- Structure and plan the session. Balance the time between presentation of information and time for discussion. Explain your structure and schedule to the group, that is: starting at… due to finish at… topics today… (make your list of the points that must be presented to remind yourself).
- Establish what the participants already understand about weight loss and find out about progress (if any) with their weight loss.
- Decide what visual aids you will use (posters? leaflets?). Are they easy to read; do they make the points that you need to present to the group? Can the women personalise this information, by making their own notes on the leaflets?
- Plan for a conclusion, which should include feedback time and questions or activities to establish what participants have learned.

Activity 4.5 (page 65)

You will need to think carefully about this apparently easy activity. Maximising the effectiveness of this resource and opportunity for the department to put across important health messages will involve some thought and planning.

- Is the new display stand in its final resting place in the clinic or do you see an alternative location? Will this new position mean better access for patients in the waiting area? Will the new proposed location meet with health and safety requirements, for example it must not block access to fire exits?
- What are the types of clinics that run in this area of outpatients? Check out the weekly timetable for the clinics. If there are a number of different clinics running over the week you may choose to display a variety of leaflets; alternatively you may want to propose to your mentor that the department selects a 'theme' that runs for a period of time. (There is a need to change a 'theme' regularly so that looking at the same materials doesn't become boring.) If, however, the area always has a regular clinic running in the location, for example cardiology, selection of the patient information leaflets should be focused on linked topics.
- Plan to spend time looking through the new materials that have been ordered for the display stand; ask your mentor about this access. Look at the 'Top tips' again for ideas (given earlier).
- Select from the resource box the PILs for the display stand; count them out (this keeps a crude estimate of numbers of patients acquiring the leaflets). Work out a proposed top-up system for replacing removed leaflets.
- Put the selected leaflets out before clinics start.
- Discuss with your mentor your approach to this work.

Further reading

Department of Health (2003) *Toolkit for Producing Patient Information*. London: DH. Available from **www.dh.gov.uk/prod_consum_dh/groups/dh_digitalassets/@dh/@en/documents/digitalasset/dh_4068462.pdf**

Department of Health (2004) *Providing Patients with Better Information in Emergency Departments – Toolkit* (Electronic only). London: DH. Available from **www.dh.gov.uk/en/Publicationsandstatistics/Publications/PublicationsPolicyAndGuidance/DH_4081347**

Patient Education and Counseling
The official journal of EACH, the European Association for Communication in Healthcare and AACH, the American Academy on Communication in Healthcare. It is an interdisciplinary, international journal for patient education and health promotion researchers, managers, physicians, nurses and other healthcare providers. It has articles which are not always easy-to-read as the contributors write in an academic and research-based style. American nurse researchers lead the field in patient education. It is worth reading though, to see many ideas for teaching patients, and to realise the strength of research internationally.

Useful websites

www.patient.co.uk/pils.asp
www.netdoctor.co.uk/
www.healthtalkonline.org
www.besthealth.bmj.com

You may like to look at some of the websites that patients can access for information. These have a range of health news, electronic leaflets and information videos on medical conditions and health problems. These websites are recommended because they give reliable health information; be cautious about using sites sponsored by health products. The health charity websites are also useful and reliable: look up the website for the patient support you are interested in, such as breast cancer.

Chapter 5
Supporting self-management

NMC Standards for Pre-registration Nursing Education

This chapter will address the following competencies:

Domain 1: Professional values

4. All nurses must work in partnership with service users, carers, families, groups, communities and organisations. They must manage risk, and promote health and wellbeing while aiming to empower choices that promote self-care and safety.

Domain 3: Nursing practice and decision-making

8. All nurses must provide educational support, facilitation skills and therapeutic nursing interventions to optimise health and wellbeing. They must promote self-care and management wherever possible, helping people to make choices about their healthcare needs, involving families and carers where appropriate, to maximise their ability to care for themselves.

NMC Essential Skills Clusters

This chapter will address the following ESCs:

Cluster: Care, compassion and communication

2. People can trust the newly registered graduate nurse to engage in person-centred care empowering people to make choices about how their needs are met when they are unable to meet them for themselves.

By the first progression point:

1. Takes a person-centred, personalised approach to care.

By the second progression point:

2. Actively empowers people to be involved in the assessment and care planning process.
4. Actively supports people in their own care and self care.
5. Considers with the person and their carers their capability for self care.

By entry to the register:

8. Is sensitive and empowers people to meet their own needs and make choices and considers with the person and their carer(s) their capability to care.
9. Ensures access to independent advocacy.
10. Recognises situations and acts appropriately when a person's choice may compromise their safety or the safety of others.
11. Uses strategies to manage situations where a person's wishes conflict with nursing interventions necessary for the person's safety.
14. Actively helps people to identify and use their strengths to achieve their goal and aspirations.

Introduction

Self-management of long-term conditions is at the heart of current health policy, urging healthcare professionals to support and help people with long-term conditions to take control of those conditions. Nurses have been identified by the government as the key professionals to give such help.

This chapter will outline the concept of self-management and epidemiological data of long-term conditions. It will also discuss various models of self-management and relevant health policy which nurses can use as a framework to build self-management programmes. In doing so, nurses are aiming to support patients to take responsibility for their own health by developing decision-making skills, the ability to work collaboratively with healthcare practitioners and being able to set realistic daily personal plans to enhance their quality of life. The chapter will also address the ethical issues which nurses have to consider when they are involved in the promotion of self-management for patients with long-term conditions.

Case study

Annie, who is 45 years old, describes herself as youthful looking, stylish and eloquent. She was diagnosed with Crohn's disease ten years ago. At the time, she was working as a secondary school teacher and was a single mother of two children. She and her husband had divorced the year before her diagnosis. Recently, Annie became an expert patients' educator for Crohn's disease. During one of the sessions she delivered to a group of ten participants, all of them suffering with the same condition, Annie reminisces:

> *When first I was diagnosed with Crohn's disease I had problems of accepting my diagnosis and re-adjusting my lifestyle. I felt very anxious and fearful about my future. I was in turmoil about whether to share my health news with my children. I was fearful of how this could affect our relationship. I kept it to myself for one year. Eventually the time came to speak to them. They both used the internet and found out everything one can about Crohn's disease. The children are a great support. However, Crohn's took over our lives.*

Annie recalls that she was losing her self-confidence and self-esteem. She started to lose control of her life and eventually she lost her job.

continued overleaf...

continued...

> *I thought that I would be teaching until retirement age. In the early days I felt constantly worn out and depressed. I could not go out unless I knew that I could access toilet facilities immediately when the need arose. I used to dread when I had to visit my gastroenterology consultant. As soon as I entered the door of the consultation room I used to feel like a six-year-old going to see the head teacher. I used to feel very vulnerable and completely disempowered. He had complete control over the management of my condition. He was making all the decisions based on the medical presentation and his professional expertise. For example, on each visit he would always ascertain how often I opened my bowels daily and then he would proceed to readjust my medication. At the time I felt that my consultant did not value my personal experience and expertise which I had developed over time about Crohn's disease. My dream was that one day I would walk into the consultation room and be able to deal with the situation better. I wanted to be heard and to participate in the decision-making process about my own health. I wanted to be acknowledged as myself and not as the person with Crohn's.*

Self-management

During your clinical experience you may have seen cases similar to Annie's. This case study clearly illustrates that Annie, in the early days of her journey with Crohn's, did not have any control over the management of her condition. It also highlights her desire to be an active participant in the decision-making process. She explicitly wanted to be in charge of her life and own health. The case study raises many pertinent issues (lack of control and confidence, vulnerability, non-participation in decision-making and unequal power between professionals and patients) which have a huge impact on the life and health outcomes of individuals who suffer with long-term conditions.

In your career so far you may have observed that while drugs are necessary in the management of illness, they offer only partial solutions to the problem and to the medical management of chronic conditions. Annie clearly wanted to take back some control over her life. She did not want Crohn's disease to dominate her life and the life of her children. She wanted to gain her own personal identity and dignity.

The case study illustrates succinctly the medicalisation of health in the early years of Annie's condition. The focus was on controlling the disease rather than on the promotion of good health and wellbeing as advocated by the NMC. The doctor is in charge and the patient is a passive, docile and obedient participant. However, current clinical practice is changing under the influence of evolved cultural and professional values and government policy. The Department of Health aims to improve the health of people who suffer with long-term diseases by urging local community health organisations to empower patients by implementing health promotion strategies which encourage self-management.

Self-management as a concept is geared towards people who are suffering with long-term conditions, for example diabetes, Crohn's, arthritis and asthma, as well as their carers and families. It aims to increase patients' independence by improving their quality of life. It also aims to enable them to be active and productive citizens by taking control of their own health and personal life. This means that you, as a nurse, should undertake health promotion interventions (see the section 'Models of self-management' later in this chapter) which enable your patients with long-term health conditions to maximise their health potential and quality of life rather than just to control and manage their illness. Your patients have to develop self-reliance mechanisms by being proactive rather than passive recipients of healthcare. They have to find solutions to everyday problems and not submit to a life which is dominated by their disease. As a nurse in partnership with other professionals, you are a key player in facilitating this transition.

Epidemiological evidence supporting self-management

Activity 5.1   *Critical thinking*

As a student nurse you will have nursed patients who suffered with a variety of long-term conditions under the supervision of your mentor.

- Note down some of the conditions you have come across during your clinical experience.
- Consider what many of these patients have in common.

There is an outline answer for this activity at the end of the chapter.

In the UK life expectancy improved steadily over the twentieth century and continues to do so. It is estimated that women born between 2004 and 2006 will live on average to 81 years of age while men will reach the age of 77 years.

Living longer is good news. However, as we live longer, the chances of developing diseases which will have a long-term effect on our health such as arthritis, heart conditions, diabetes and respiratory problems to mention a few, are increasing for both sexes. The conditions are a threat to health status and cause impairment to the quality of life due to disability.

It is estimated that today in the UK an alarming 17.5 million adults are living with a long-term condition (DH, 2005). The Department of Health estimates that 45% of those who suffer with long-term conditions will suffer from more than one condition, e.g. a person with diabetes may also have circulatory and ophthalmic problems. This increased prevalence of long-term conditions results in the following:

- an increased number of hospital admissions and long hospitalisation, accounting for 70% of hospital bed occupancy;
- an increased number of consultations with GPs, responsible for 50% of all GP consultations;
- in England the overall NHS expenditure on the care and treatment of long-term conditions accounts for 70% of total allocated NHS budget;
- people with long-terms conditions have increased levels of absenteeism from work;
- long-term conditions are more prevalent amongst the lower socio-economic groups (lower income).

These national statistics are supported by the WHO, which forecasts that if long-term diseases are not successfully managed by 2020 they will be the most expensive problem for healthcare systems across the world. Long-term health problems are costly both in terms of the medical care needed and in the loss of national productivity because of time off work. A long-term condition is also a great burden to the individual as it causes both physical suffering and social disadvantage. As a practitioner at the front line of healthcare provision, you will have to tackle these problems by being the steering force for implementing self-management initiatives at the grass roots of clinical practice. You therefore need to re-orientate your clinical practice from a 'disease management' to a 'health enhancing' approach.

You need to act as a facilitator, which means that you have to develop new skills and to adopt a new culture of practice with the appropriate attitudes and behaviours to support patients to be independent and self-caring (see Chapters 7 and 8).

Health policy context of self-management for chronic conditions

Current government policy provides nurses with a framework and guidance on how to accomplish this transformation of practice. The government document *High Quality Care for All: The next stage review final report* (DH, 2008b) sets out the agenda for self-management. It states that the NHS has to focus not only on the treatment of disease but also on health improvement. The subsequent two documents *Your Health, Your Way: a guide to long-term conditions and self-care* (DH, 2009b) and *Improving the Health and Well Being of People with Long-term Conditions* (DH, 2010b) provide further evidence for the implementation of a self-management approach by healthcare professionals.

These policies aim to produce better health outcomes and improve the quality of life of people with long-term conditions, slow the progression of their condition and reduce disability. In order to achieve their aims they embrace the concept of self-management by endorsing the Ottawa Charter Principles (WHO, 1986) as discussed in Chapter 1.

The Department of Health identifies nurses as the key professionals responsible to provide health promotion intervention to enable patients to self-manage the complexities of their conditions. The above-mentioned health strategies in conjunction with NICE guidelines and national service frameworks (NSFs) (diabetes, cancer, mental health, long-term conditions) provide nurses with a framework which informs and shapes the development of a 'self-management practice'.

Underpinning principles of supporting self-management for long-term conditions

Activity 5.2   *Reflection and critical thinking*

Reflect on three patients with three different chronic conditions who you have nursed during your clinical placements, e.g. patients suffering with arthritis, diabetes and Parkinson's disease. Now consider the therapeutic conversations you have had with them and their families. What were their expressed views? For example:

- Were they happy to be in hospital?
- What health information did they receive and from whom?
- Were they satisfied with the health information they received?
- Did they feel that NHS provision at the local level met their needs?
- Did they receive any professional support when they were discharged home?
- How did the professionals who care for them encourage self-management?

There is an outline answer for this activity at the end of the chapter.

Reflecting on the activity, you may conclude that the conversations revealed the following common principles:

- Patients taking responsibility for their own health management: how can you facilitate this? Is the state discharging responsibility to the individual?
- Patients feeling confident in their own ability to take control of their own health: how can you promote self-efficacy? Do you need to address health inequalities? Have patients the ability and knowledge to solve health problems? Can they be trusted that they will do the right thing? What is your role and the role of the other health professionals? (see Chapter 1).
- Nurses respecting and valuing patients' personal experience and knowledge of their own illness: can lay knowledge have equal credibility and validity to professional expert knowledge?

These principles echo the underpinning principles of the self-management concept. It also indicates that nurses need to clarify their professional accountability and redefine the nursing role.

You need to be able to behave in a different way in pursuing a practice which promotes self-management for long-term conditions.

- Establish an ongoing good interactive relationship with your patients and their families and carers, which is built on mutual respect and trust. Provide them with the opportunity to discuss anxieties, worries and concerns with you. However, do not assume that lay people believe that professionals know best. Patients sometimes receive conflicting and contradictory advice from professionals such as on the issue of dairy foods affecting Crohn's disease.
- Develop a personalised self-management plan (see Chapter 7). Patients are entering into an equal partnership with healthcare professionals. Health outcomes and realistic goals are set by negotiation and mutual agreement. Progress is reviewed constantly by both parties. You

need to ensure that agreement is reached by patients exercising autonomy, freedom of choice and voluntary consent.

- Make sure that you deliver patient-centred education. Educational activities should be sensitive to cultural diversity and individual values and beliefs. You have to be prepared to encounter negative feelings from some patients who may resent and reject your health advice on the basis that they are 'being told what to do'. They may feel frustrated and find it difficult to conform and change their behaviour due to socio-economic factors such as lack of money or job opportunities. This highlights the importance of devising a truly personalised education which is tailor-made to patients' individual life circumstances and personal attributes and builds on their strengths and weakness.
- Gain active patient participation in the decision-making process by building patients' confidence and self-esteem and sustaining motivation. Ensure that every patient feels confident and competent to put the advice into practice by the development of skills such as a diabetic patient becoming able to re-adjust their insulin dosage when they meet friends socially over drinks. However, you need to consider whether patients have the cognitive and emotional skills to make informed decisions. You need to question what opportunities patients have to influence care policy and guidelines. It may be said by professionals that they welcome patients' views, but much consultation is really only placatory.
- Enable patients to take responsibility and control of their own health by developing problem-solving skills. You should not assume that all patients want to be responsible for their health at all times. Due to changes in personal circumstances due to a 'flare up' of their condition, patients will feel very ill, vulnerable and unable to cope. They may feel despondent and disheartened and they may rely on the professionals to make decisions on their behalf. Development of coping skills is at the heart of self-management, as you are aiming to transform your patient from a sufferer to a manager.

Nurses involved in supporting patients to self-manage their long-term conditions must consider these ways of working. Patients' autonomy, freedom of choice, voluntarism, participation in decision-making, responsibility and the ability to take control of their own health is the essence of health promotion practice. Patients, their families and significant others are viewed as your equal partners.

Models of self-management education

When supporting patients to self-manage their condition, how do you structure and shape your health promotion practice? As seen earlier, health policy will be instrumental in guiding your practice. Additionally, nurses, in collaboration with other health professionals, can facilitate the process of self-management by adopting the following models:

- expert patient programme;
- structured education programmes such as for diabetes;
- empowerment.

All of these models incorporate many common activities based in health promotion theory (Chapter 1) which aim to support and help patients to take control of their condition and to promote good health.

In the UK, these models have informed the design of many self-management programmes such as for diabetes, substance and alcohol misuse, and pain.

Have you noticed that self-management is a tertiary level prevention, as identified by Tannahill (1986) (see Chapter 1)? The patients already have the disease and you aim to support and facilitate them to cope with their disease and to improve their quality of life. However, as a nurse you have to remember that not all patients with long-term conditions will have the same level of health needs (Chapter 7).

Even though all models have the same core aim(s) and they utilise the similar health promotion theory, they differ in terms of who is involved in their delivery.

Expert Patients Programme (EPP)

Case study: Expert Patients Programme

Mick is a 67-year-old gentleman who has suffered from arthritis for the past 35 years. He is a retired self-employed gas central heating engineer. He has been married to Monica for 45 years and has two sons and two grandsons. Mick's main hobbies are sailing and ballroom dancing.

Despite suffering pain and experiencing various degrees of stiffness and difficulty in using his hands, he worked until retirement age. He has been able to adapt and manage his arthritis with the support of his wife, consultant, physiotherapist, GP and practice nurse.

During a routine consultation with the practice nurse he was told about the Expert Patients Programme. He recalls:

> *I got very excited as I felt that I had all the qualifications to be a peer educationalist. I like talking to and interacting with people of all cultures through my work and not to forget that I suffer from arthritis for 35 years.*

> *I registered to attend a local course run by my PCT in a church hall near the town centre. I enjoyed the course and I found it fascinating. I learned a lot and I found that the participants had many things in common. Things such as taking painkillers before exercise activity, writing down questions to ask during GP visits and remembering to take prescriptions on holiday.*

Mick attended the EPP course and he is now a voluntary peer educator, helping to run other courses. He evaluated the course as follows:

> *The EPP gave me the licence to make informed decisions for myself. It built up my in-depth knowledge and understanding about my medication and potential complications of my condition. The course had a generic approach to fit with everybody's needs. One has to appreciate that the participants are at different stages with their condition. I learned how important it is to accept my condition (as there is no other alternative). Now I have learned to ventilate my feelings. I used to get on with things until I couldn't cope, while now I find it easy to express my own feelings to others. I no longer feel isolated.*

He enjoys being a volunteer peer educator:

continued overleaf...

continued...

As a peer educator I feel that I can share my personal experience and learning with others. This is important as a lot of the things we (patients) experience are common to us all, even though we may suffer with different conditions. I am able to support and help other people. When a participant has a problem we discuss this as a group and all of us make suggestions how to deal with it.

Each week we set achievable, realistic goals for participants. The course allows people to have realistic expectations from themselves, e.g. you can exercise by taking the grandchildren for a walk in the park instead of expecting to run a marathon! It encourages participants to do something for themselves rather than expect professionals or the system to do it for them.

EPP can be a social event and it helps you to have a laugh without undermining the seriousness of the course.

The case study gives a succinct account of the EPP concept and highlights how it supports patients to self-manage their long-term conditions. It is important to realise that the EPP is taught by lay people who have long-term conditions themselves: peer education is a key part of the model. People are given training to enable them to teach groups and there is a system of support for them to perform this role.

The Expert Patients Programme is a government initiative which has the support and recognition of the WHO. Since 2002, following the recommendations of the Wanless (2002) report, it is delivered as a free programme by the NHS for people who suffer with a long-term conditions. However, its origins can be traced back to the 1990s, when the voluntary sector introduced the notion of lay-led self-management for chronic conditions. Currently, EPP courses are provided by over half of local community health organisations in England. The EPP is also provided by all local health boards in Wales and is part of the health policy for Scotland.

The Arthritis Self-Management Programme is considered to be the prototype of the EPP self-management course, dating back to 1979. It is a community-based programme for people who suffer with rheumatoid arthritis, osteoarthritis, lupus and fibromyalgia. The programme has been evaluated over the years using randomised trials. The evaluation results indicate that participants reduced their pain, sometimes their disability, reduced the uptake of NHS services and overall improved their quality of life (Lorig et al., 1993).

The Substance and Alcohol Misuse (SAM) course is another example of an EPP programme. It offers people who are recovering from drug and alcohol misuses the opportunity to learn skills which enable them to integrate successfully back into the community. This is achieved by raising participants' self-confidence, morale and sustaining their motivation to change. The course teaches them a variety of techniques which enables them to organise their day-to-day activities constructively by setting realistic goals and making action plans. It provides participants with valuable tools and techniques which enable them to improve communication with their families, friends and healthcare professionals and to gain the necessary skills to seek paid or voluntary employment or to pursue further education.

There are EPP programmes for general groups of patients, for those with conditions such as pain, and for carers. It is offered in modified forms to meet the needs of young people and people with learning difficulties.

Evaluation of the EPP is positive. It indicates that participants can improve their quality of life and minimise deterioration of their condition. They are able to adopt healthy lifestyles (better diet and increase physical activity), to try new things and make important life-changing decisions because the course has increased their self-awareness and self-worth. However, evaluation has also indicated some shortcomings in relation to clinical management of diseases, for example patients with diabetes have not always been able to control effectively their diabetes or their diet. This highlights the need for patient education programmes which are led by professional experts (Cabe et al., 2006).

Structured education programmes for long-term conditions

Structured educational programmes are set up by care services for patients with certain conditions and offered to patients and carers. They are run by healthcare professionals who have professional expertise and experience pertinent to the long-term condition in question. The educators are mainly nurse specialists, practice nurses, physiotherapists and dieticians. However, other healthcare professionals may be involved, depending on the nature of the condition, such as podiatrists, pharmacists, physiotherapists and doctors.

Examples of structured education programmes include:

- DAFNE (Dose Adjustment for Normal Eating) – for those with insulin-dependent diabetes
- DESMOND (Diabetes Education and Self Management for Ongoing and Newly Diagnosed) – for those with non-insulin-dependent diabetes;
- X-PERT – for those with diabetes (not the same as the EPP);
- Challenging Your Condition – for those with arthritis.

Others are set up when health professionals consider there is a need. The names of some programmes are often made up locally; even the diabetes programmes may be redesigned for local use and given a local name such as BERTIE in Bournemouth and WINDFAL at the Whittington hospital, London.

The programmes are structured to support patients in self-managing their condition. Their curricula are provided by professionals and designed to meet the standards of self-management as outlined in the policies discussed previously. This ensures uniformity of all programmes irrespective of where they are delivered as they meet and fulfil national standards. This also enhances participants' confidence that they are attending approved, worthwhile programmes.

It is estimated that these programmes are the preferred choice of the majority of healthcare organisations throughout the UK in their effort to promote self-management among patients suffering with long-term conditions. They are delivered predominately in local community health organisations, for example in a community health centre, though some are offered in hospitals by their specialist teams. Nurses caring for patients need to be aware of the availability of relevant local programmes, their start dates and venues, in order to arrange for patients to attend.

Typically, they run over a number of weeks (often six weeks) and each session is of two to three hours' duration. The sessions are interactive and each group consists of approximately ten participants.

The curricula usually address three areas:

- medical management of the condition – for example, participants will be educated on how to manage their medication and how to monitor their peak flow or blood glucose levels;
- role management – for example, delegation of responsibility to others, asking a partner to do the weekly shopping;
- emotional management: coping with anger, fatigue.

Inherent to the education programme is the development of problem-solving skills, decision-making, resource utilisation, forming a partnership with the health professionals and taking actions in reasonable steps (action planning). This can be illustrated in the following case study.

Case study: A structured education model

Olu is a 56-year-old man who suffers with hypertension. He is employed and often works up to 50 hours per week. Because of work pressures, he eats a lot of fast food for convenience. He cannot reduce his weight as he does not have time to exercise. Since his diagnosis two years ago, he is worried that he may die of a heart attack. He takes his own blood pressure readings but because of work commitment, he finds it difficult to visit his GP. Recently his blood pressure readings were constantly elevated. His wife made an appointment for him to see his GP. During the consultation he was advised to see the practice nurse with a view to enrolling on the structured patient education programme run by the practice nurse for hypertensive patients. Olu was seen by the practice nurse and arrangements were made to attend the course. After completion of the course Olu was able to self-manage his hypertension by the development of the following skills:

- *Problem-solving: he is able to follow and adhere to a care plan which was agreed between himself and his GP, practice nurse, pharmacist and dietician. He now checks and records his blood pressure readings regularly. He also takes a small cooler bag to work which he packs with his lunch.*
- *Decision-making: he has negotiated with his employer to be transferred to another department within the company and has reduced his working hours. He has set realistic exercise goals to fit with his daily life.*
- *Using resources: Olu uses the internet to update his knowledge about hypertension. He now visits his local library and is using the library's databases for research articles.*
- *Partnership with the health professionals: at visits to the GP and practice nurse, he always uses his health diary (blood pressure recordings, medication regime and nutrition intake) to discuss his progress. He and his wife now write down a list of questions to ask the healthcare professionals.*
- *Action planning: Olu ensures that he stays healthy by adopting a healthy lifestyle and reducing his stress levels by taking time out to relax. He has set goals to improve his eating and exercise behaviour, and he has a weekly plan.*

The structured patient education model allows health professionals to design a curriculum for learning knowledge and skills and developing attitudes enabling self-management. Nurses quite often meet patients who need a bit of a push to start helping themselves with their ongoing ill health condition. Some rely too much on the actions of professionals to help them, and are perhaps afraid to take charge of their lives. Patients may be reluctant to change.

Empowerment

The EPP and structured patient education programmes all empower patients and their families to take control of their long-term condition as a core aim. Empowerment is the hub of health promotion and over the last 20 years it has been seen as one of the most significant innovations in the management of long-term conditions. An empowerment approach strengthens patients' abilities to pursue effective self-management programmes. We will consider the theory supporting empowerment.

Case study: Empowerment

Robert, who is 48, is a director of his own company and lives with his wife Mary. In 1983 he was diagnosed with type 1 diabetes (insulin-dependent). As part of the initiative for involving service users in the local university's health faculty, he has been invited to speak to a group of student nurses about his health journey of living with diabetes and the progress from being a passive patient to becoming an empowered patient.

Robert tells the students:

When first diagnosed with insulin-dependent diabetes I found it very difficult to cope with the challenges of living with diabetes. I felt very frustrated and angry. I found it difficult to discuss this with my wife and this caused a strain on our relationship. I started to blame myself for my personal failing and I felt isolated.

On reflection my initial experience of managing my diabetes was overall very mechanistic and prescriptive in nature. I was following a management regime which was determined and prescribed by my consultant and his team. The health information and written materials I received were impersonal, generic and didactic. I had no autonomy. I had to adapt my lifestyle to fit my diabetic care as recommended by the healthcare professionals (consultant, nurse and dietician).

Today, in contrast, my diabetes management gives me flexibility and I can be spontaneous in my daily activities without having to think constantly about my diabetes. I feel confident and in control. My wife plays an active and supportive role. This change took place as both of us participated in a number of patient education programmes which are widely available, easily accessible, informative and non-threatening. They emphasise the role of the patient in the decision-making process and they validate our own experience and knowledge of diabetes.

Another significant change which has empowered me is the advent of a collaborative team approach to care. The healthcare team offers a wide spectrum of interprofessional expertise and experience. Nowadays, I am able to devise management plans which I can adapt to my own personal lifestyle, needs, wants and desires without compromising the fundamental medical treatment required for my diabetes.

Robert's case study reiterates that empowerment is at the hub of self-management and demonstrates how empowered patients can control their long-term conditions and can lead a fulfilled life.

Tones and Tilford (2001) provide nurses and other health professionals with an empowerment model known as Tones' empowerment model. The model is widely used in the promotion of self-management. It illustrates that health education leads to empowerment and is based on the notion that the acquisition of health knowledge and skills which are sensitive to the individual's culture, values and beliefs can raise an individual's **critical consciousness**. This is a term first used by the Brazilian educationalist Paulo Freire; critical consciousness is the level at which an individual is able to view objectively the reality of his health status. They have the confidence, self-esteem and self-efficacy to challenge the politics of health and achieve political change, leading to an equitable and holistic health. In the case of self-management, a knowledgeable patient can influence health policy at the local and national level. Robert is able to debate and adapt his diabetes management, and he is beginning also to contribute to local health planning decisions for diabetes patients.

In your clinical experience as a student nurse, you may have encountered examples of self-management which are based on the philosophy of the empowerment concept, for example patients with severe pain taking control over their pain management via 'patient controlled analgesia' known as PCA in surgical wards. This is a system whereby post-operative patients can self-control the dosage of analgesia they receive according to their pain levels by pressing a button which activates an electronically controlled pump to inject a prescribed opioid analgesic into their vein. Similarly, in the medical wards patients can self-administer their medication. Nurses play an active role in this, as each patient has to fulfil all the criteria for self-administration, as stated by local and national protocols. The nurse in collaboration with the patient reviews daily the self-management plan.

How empowered do you think your patients feel? Do you think that patients have the same understanding of empowerment as the health professionals? The case study evaluates the empowerment model of self-management very positively with a high level of satisfaction and great enhancement of Robert's quality of life. This is very much in accordance with the literature, which reveals that empowerment benefits patients who are at the higher levels of the social spectrum.

We know that patients who are at a greater socio-economic disadvantage (see inequalities in health in Chapter 6) tend not to be so empowered and are also less inclined to seek empowerment. The idea that the professionals know best, that there is little the individual can do to help themselves, can be quite a barrier to developing self-management skills. To reach a level of critical consciousness may be a longer term goal for these patients and therefore the nurses caring for them. Perhaps we need to think about a beginner level of health literacy at first (see Chapter 4).

Chapter summary

This chapter has enabled you to explore and develop your understanding of the need to support patients to self-manage their long-term conditions. It has also enabled you to use epidemiological evidence as a rationale to develop nursing practice which promotes patients' health and enhances their quality of life. Your practice has to be informed by current health policy and apply the principles of expert patient programmes, structured patient education programmes and empowerment. The chapter has encouraged you to critically evaluate their effectiveness as well as to consider your changing role in your efforts to support patients to self-manage their chronic conditions.

Activities: Brief outline answers

Activity 5.1 (page 75)

The list is not exhaustive. It may include: arthritis, asthma, chronic obstructive pulmonary disease, ulcerative colitis, Crohn's disease, diabetes (types 1 and 2), hypothyroidism, epilepsy, HIV/AIDS, Parkinson's disease, multiple sclerosis, cancers, and mental health problems such as alcohol and substance abuse.

Many patients with long-term or chronic conditions have similar problems with:

- pain;
- limited mobility;
- sleep problems;
- depression;
- lack of social activities;
- difficulties with social support;
- eating or weight difficulties.

Activity 5.2 (page 77)

You may have found that the majority of them had similar views and needs, independent of their condition.

The majority of patients prefer to come to hospital only if it is absolutely necessary, in which case they would prefer to be a planned admission.

Most of patients may have received health information from nurses and other health professionals on lifestyle issues, i.e. exercises, diet, alcohol.

Overall, patients want to have good, high-quality, simple information.

They may want to have easy access to information to enable them to be more independent and proactive about their self-care and management of their own health.

Many may have expressed the need to have more support in the community, for example helplines (run by professionals specialising in their condition) to seek support and advice as and when they need.

They want user-friendly and easily accessible NHS services, for example GP surgeries to have longer opening hours.

Further reading

Department of Health (2007) *Supporting People with Long-term Conditions to Self Care.* London: DH.
A guide to supporting people with long-term conditions to self-manage through an integrated package which includes information, self-monitoring devices, self-care skills education and training and self-care support networks.

Embrey, N (2006) A concept analysis of self-management in long-term conditions. *British Journal of Neuroscience Nursing,* 2,(10): 507–13, available on **www.internurse.com/cgi-bin/go.pl/library/ article.cgi?uid=22535;article=BJNN_2_10_507_513**
An analysis of the concept of self-management, theoretical but very useful in reviewing exactly what it entails.

Useful websites

www.expertpatients.co.uk/
Website of the Expert Patients Programme, a community interest company.

www.dafne.uk.com/
Website of the DAFNE structured diabetes education programme.

www.desmond-project.org.uk/
Website of the DESMOND structured diabetes education programme.

Chapter 6
Considering public health

NMC Standards for Pre-registration Nursing Education

This chapter will address the following competencies:

Domain 1: Professional values

3. All nurses must support and promote the health, wellbeing, rights and dignity of people, groups, communities and populations. These include people whose lives are affected by ill health, disability, ageing, death and dying. Nurses must understand how these activities influence public health.

Domain 3: Nursing practice and decision-making

Generic standard for competence

... All nurses must also understand how behaviour, culture, socioeconomic and other factors, in the care environment and its location, can affect health, illness, health outcomes and public health priorities and take this into account in planning and delivering care.

5. All nurses must understand public health principles, priorities and practice in order to recognise and respond to the major causes and social determinants of health, illness and health inequalities. They must use a range of information and data to assess the needs of people, groups, communities and populations, and work to improve health, wellbeing and experiences of healthcare; secure equal access to health screening, health promotion and healthcare; and promote social inclusion.

NMC Essential Skills Clusters

This chapter will address the following ESCs:

Cluster: Organisational aspects of care

9. People can trust the newly registered graduate nurse to treat them as partners and work with them to make a holistic and systematic assessment of their needs; to develop a personalised plan that is based on mutual understanding and respect for their individual situation promoting health and well-being, minimising risk of harm and promoting their safety at all times.

By the second progression point:

3. Understands the concept of public health and the benefits of healthy lifestyles and the potential risks involved with various lifestyles or behaviours, for example, substance misuse, smoking, obesity.

18. Discusses sensitive issues in relation to public health and provides appropriate advice and guidance to individuals, communities and populations for example, contraception, substance misuse, smoking, obesity.

continued overleaf...

continued...

22. Works within a public health framework to assess needs and plan care for individuals, communities and populations.

Cluster: Infection prevention and control

21. People can trust the newly registered graduate nurse to identify and take effective measures to prevent and control infection in accordance with local and national policy.

By the second progression point:

6. Discusses the benefits of health promotion within the concept of public health in the prevention and control of infection for improving and maintaining the health of the population.

By entry to the register:

11. Recognises infection risk and reports and acts in situations where there is need for health promotion and protection and public health strategies.

Chapter aims

By the end of the chapter you will be able to:

- understand the scope of public health;
- describe the structure of public health functions in the UK;
- appreciate the role of the nurse in the control of communicable diseases;
- recognise the need to respond to public health emergencies.

Introduction

Public health is an overall term which covers aspects of disease prevention and health promotion, and is a broader term than treatments or care for people who are ill. Although much of what we do as nurses falls under the meaning of public health, it is not often recognised as such. Nurses get involved with preventing disease through immunisation and screening, but this is only part of our public health role. Their knowledge of the causes and population patterns of disease is helpful to nurses' understanding of why people become ill.

Most nurses, however, do not see themselves as public health practitioners. The Nursing and Midwifery Council have set up a specialist register for nurses working in this area which currently includes:

- health visiting;
- occupational health;
- school nursing;
- sexual health;
- health protection;
- family health nursing in Scotland.

The government intends to strengthen the public health function of nurses (Department of Health, 2010a). You need to be aware that there is an increasing need for nurses to develop understanding of and skills in public health practice even if you are not going to be on the specialist NMC register.

Recent outbreaks of various types of influenza (pandemic flu, avian flu) have shown that the public turn to nurses among other health professionals for reassurance and information. The current issue of children as young as 14 developing what used to be called elder-onset (type 2, non-insulin-dependent) diabetes should indicate to you that knowledge of disease causes and trends will help you understand and keep up with changes in health care practice.

What is public health?

Public health can be seen as a very general term to include all aspects of health – some writers use the term this way, which can be confusing. On the other hand public health can be seen as everything except the treatment and care aspects of health – some writers use it to describe prevention of disease and promotion of health.

> ### Concept summary: Definitions of public health
>
> The usual definition in government documents and used by the Faculty of Public Health is: *the science and art of preventing disease, prolonging life and promoting health through the organised efforts of society* (Acheson, 1988).

The current public health white paper (Department of Health, 2010a) also uses this definition and goes on to propose that this government will expect the outcomes of public health practice to be in five areas (domains):

1. health protection and resilience: protecting people from major health emergencies and serious harm to health;
2. tackling the wider determinants of ill health: addressing factors that affect health and wellbeing;
3. health improvement: positively promoting the adoption of 'healthy' lifestyles;
4. prevention of ill health: reducing the number of people living with preventable ill health;
5. healthy life expectancy and preventable mortality: preventing people from dying prematurely.

Note that health promotion (quite commonly called health improvement) is a part of public health. Public health also addresses the factors causing disease and death.

Health promotion makes up a small part of all outcomes public health's outcomes

Who does public health?

There is currently a government-linked organisation called the Health Protection Agency (not part of the Department of Health) whose role is to provide an integrated approach to protecting UK public health through the provision of support and advice to the Department of Health, the

National Health Service, local authorities, and other health-related organisations. The agency is responsible for advice in the following areas:

- infectious (communicable) diseases – such as influenza (flu), HIV, health care associated infections (MRSA);
- radiation – mobile phones, radon, WiFi;
- chemicals and poisons – chemical hazards, poisons information service;
- emergency response – extreme weather events, deliberate releases.

Activity 6.1   *Critical thinking*

Go to the Health Protection Agency website and look up a topic which interests you. Have a look at the front page of the website for news first, particularly if there is a health crisis such as an epidemic or a heatwave happening at the time. Then use the site search engine to look up something either to do with your current practice area or something which you are curious about. Here are some suggestions:

- MMR vaccine;
- Olympics;
- antibiotic resistance;
- leprosy;
- meningitis;
- E. Coli.

There is no further guidance on this activity as it is to raise your interest in how public health works.

The current coalition government has recently decided to restructure public health and in its white paper (DH, 2010a) proposed the setting up of a new organisation to be called Public Health England. As you can see the white paper is for England but the Department of Health continues to work closely with the devolved administrations of Scotland, Wales and Northern Ireland. The names of organisations and the local ways of working may vary but the whole UK will be working towards the same goals in public health.

In England, Directors of Public Health will be employed by the local authorities and will be the strategic leaders for public health and health inequalities. They will work in partnership with the local NHS and across the public, private and voluntary sectors. Public Health England will be part of the Department of Health and will work for emergency preparedness and health protection. It will also hold evidence for best practice in public health, including how to change people's health behaviour. This government has undertaken to set aside a special budget for the prevention of disease including crisis management, which cannot be used for treatment and care, as they feel this is so important for health in the future.

Main issues in public health

It is simpler to think of the work of public health professionals as divided into communicable (infectious, e.g. measles) and non-communicable (e.g. diabetes) disease prevention. They also seek to prevent harm from other less predictable occurrences such as radiation leaks and poisons, as you can see from the work of the Health Protection Agency. For both communicable and non-communicable diseases it is possible to find statistics on epidemiology – the study of determinants (causes) and distribution (who gets the diseases and where) of each disease.

This is called disease surveillance and it is carried out by the public health system. Doctors in general practice and in hospitals send reports of their diagnoses to the local directors of public health and the statistics are collated by the health observatories, which are able to help the health service plan for the future using the trends in diseases.

There are several ways to find health statistics:

- use the national statistics database available on **www.statistics.gov.uk** – this website holds all national statistics on all topics including health;
- go to the website of your local community health organisation as they have to produce an annual report on the health of the area;
- look at the local health profiles compiled by the public health observatories, available on **www.apho.org.uk**;
- if you want international statistics, use the WHO at **www.who.int**;
- use a search engine such as Google and type in the name of the disease you are interested in, plus statistics.

Activity 6.2   *Critical thinking*

Using one or more of the methods above, find statistics on two diseases – one communicable, e.g. tuberculosis or HIV, and one non-communicable, e.g. asthma or depression.

Find out who is affected more – some diseases will show greater differences between:

- men and women;
- age groups;
- social classes or income levels;
- geographical locations;
- ethnic groups.

There is no further guidance on this activity as it is to raise your awareness of availability of epidemiological information.

This activity should show you that in some diseases there are obvious differences. However, in others the differences may not be so obvious and the disease is generally spread across the population.

In communicable diseases the rate and distribution of cases is related to how the infection has spread. This will not show up so much in statistical tables, but on maps and in the numbers of new cases occurring each day.

Communicable diseases

> ### Case study: Severe acute respiratory syndrome (SARS)
>
> *This communicable disease was first recognised in Guandong Province, China, in November 2002. On 12 March 2003 the WHO issued the first global alert. Three days later they sent out a second alert with guidance to health professionals and alerting international travellers. Within four months, transmission of the SARS virus had been interrupted in all the affected countries. By 5 July 2003 the outbreak had been contained.*
>
> *There were 8098 cases in 26 countries, and 774 people died. There was disruption to travel, trade and production. China was criticised for not cooperating with WHO and failure to report cases.*
>
> *Because the outbreak originated in China there was public avoidance of any Chinese residential areas in several countries, even when there were no cases there. Facemasks were widely worn in spite of questionable evidence of their effectiveness. GPs in the UK were inundated with queries about cold-like symptoms, immunisation (there is none), and demands for antibiotics (not effective against viruses). Schools and workplaces were uncertain what to do.*

This was a rather dramatic story, but all epidemics of communicable diseases are tracked in the same way and nurses need to become aware of the public health actions taken. Your role in the circumstance of an epidemic such as this is to follow the story in the press and keep up to date with your employer's policies and procedures regarding the public health response. You can also look at the news and advice on the Health Protection Agency website.

Prepare yourself for your public health role so that you are able to:

- understand the risk of a person becoming infected;
- know the typical signs and symptoms;
- answer questions from patients, relatives and your local community about the risk;
- report promptly any relevant observations in your patients (e.g. raised temperature, rash) to nursing and medical staff;
- make sense of your employer's actions such as immunisation of staff and closure of beds.

Activity 6.3   *Critical thinking*

Next time you read in the newspapers or see on the television that there is an outbreak of a communicable disease, follow the story in the press.

- Where and when did it start?
- How quickly is it spreading?
- Was it spread in a local area – how?
- Or was it spread globally by people travelling?
- How is the public responding? Is there panic, misunderstanding and confusion, anger at lack of information or action?
- What is the official information to the public?

There is no further guidance for this activity; it is to encourage you to follow a health story in the press.

As you become more aware of the public health aspects of communicable disease surveillance, you will see that some diseases seem to cause more alarm than others. Some are designated 'notifiable'.

Notifiable diseases

There are some communicable diseases which are considered to be very risky to populations and outbreaks need to be monitored and controlled quickly. Nurses need to be aware of these even though the notification is done by medical practitioners mainly. Doctors have to report cases of the notifiable diseases listed, to alert public health directors and the Health Protection Agency to possible outbreaks and epidemics.

Some of these diseases occur rarely and smallpox is an example of one deemed to be wiped out globally, but look at some of the commoner diseases on the list. You may come into contact with these, be asked by people for advice or need to be on the lookout for potential cases in your nursing practice area.

Concept summary: Notifiable diseases

Diseases notifiable (to Local Authority Proper Officers) under the Health Protection (Notification) Regulations 2010.

Acute encephalitis	Acute meningitis	Acute poliomyelitis
Acute infectious hepatitis	Anthrax	Botulism
Brucellosis	Cholera	Diphtheria
Enteric fever (typhoid or paratyphoid fever)	Food poisoning	Haemolytic uraemic syndrome (HUS)
Infectious bloody diarrhoea	Invasive group A streptococcal disease and scarlet fever	Legionnaires' disease
Leprosy	Malaria	Measles
Meningococcal septicaemia	Mumps	Plague
Rabies	Rubella	SARS
Smallpox	Tetanus	Tuberculosis
Typhus	Viral haemorrhagic fever (VHF)	Whooping cough
Yellow fever		

As of April 2010, it is no longer a requirement to notify the following diseases: dysentery, ophthalmia neonatorum, leptospirosis, and relapsing fever.

As you can see, there are some very rare diseases on this list, but also some that you are more likely to encounter. The public health actions for an outbreak of any of these diseases will be similar. You need to familiarise yourself with the signs and symptoms of the most common diseases, as well as the nursing actions to be taken and the immunisations recommended to prevent outbreaks.

Immunisation

Immunisation is a primary prevention measure for some communicable diseases. The UK has a schedule of immunisation for children, people at clinical risk and the elderly. This schedule is offered free through the NHS by health visitors and general practitioners. Information for professionals and the public is available on the Department of Health website **www.dh.gov.uk**.

Concept summary: Immunisation schedule

Two months

- Diphtheria, tetanus, pertussis (whooping cough), polio and haemophilus influenza type b (Hib, a bacterial infection that can cause severe pneumonia or meningitis in young children), given as a five-in-one single jab known as DTaP/IPV/Hib.
- Pneumococcal infection.

Three months

- Five-in-one, second dose (DTaP/IPV/Hib).
- Meningitis C.

Four months

- Five-in-one, third dose (DTaP/IPV/Hib).
- Pneumococcal infection, second dose.
- Meningitis C, second dose.

Around 12 months

- Meningitis C, third dose.
- Hib, fourth dose (Hib/MenC given as a single jab).

Around 13 months

- MMR (measles, mumps and rubella), given as a single jab.
- Pneumococcal infection, third dose.

Three years and four months, or soon after

- MMR second jab.
- Diphtheria, tetanus, pertussis and polio (DtaP/IPV), given as a four-in-one pre-school booster.

continued opposite...

continued...

Around 12–13 years

- Cervical cancer (HPV) vaccine, which protects against cervical cancer (girls only): three jabs given within six months.

Around 13–18 years

- Diphtheria, tetanus and polio booster (Td/IPV), given as a single jab.

65 and over

- Flu (every year).
- Pneumococcal.

Vaccines for risk groups

People who fall into certain risk groups may be offered extra vaccines. These include vaccinations against diseases such as hepatitis B, tuberculosis (TB), seasonal flu and chickenpox.

Travel and other vaccines

There are also optional vaccines possibly free on the NHS, including travel vaccinations such as hepatitis A, typhoid and cholera.

Seasonal (yearly) flu vaccine

This is given to the following groups:

- people aged 65 years and over;
- all those aged six months or over in a clinical risk group;
- all pregnant women;
- people living in long-stay residential care homes or other long-stay care facilities where there is a risk of high morbidity and mortality;
- those who are in receipt of a carer's allowance, or those who are the main carer, or the carer of an elderly or disabled person whose welfare may be at risk if the carer falls ill;
- frontline health and social care workers.

This schedule is quite comprehensive, but as you can see, immunisation is recommended and made available, but is not compulsory for UK residents. In some countries the public health authorities demand certain immunisations, or make them compulsory for immigrants and travellers.

People need to understand the importance of protecting themselves and their children from communicable diseases, and weigh this up against the perceived dangers of immunisation itself. They may also be unaware of the beneficial effects of having most of the population immunised, which is sometimes called 'herd immunity', when outbreaks are fewer and less severe if most people are immunised.

Activity 6.4   *Communication*

Mr Watkins is 66 and has been advised by his GP to have the flu vaccine this year. Mr Watkins is worried that this will cause him to actually develop flu and he has heard stories about how it makes people feel unwell. He has also read that there are different types of flu and is puzzled as to how one vaccine could work for all of them.

- How will you put his mind at rest and how will you persuade him to take up the offer?

A brief outline answer for this activity is given at the end of the chapter.

Working through this activity may help your own decision as to whether to take up the flu vaccine as a health professional. You too need to be protected.

Public health professionals worry about people not being immunised and about herd immunity. They monitor the uptake of immunisations and set targets for local community health organisations to achieve. For the flu vaccine. estimated uptake in those aged 65 years and over is 72.8% (2009/10, 72.4%), and in the clinical risk groups under 65 years of age is 50.3% (2009/10, 51.6%); and in pregnant women is 37.7% as of 27 February 2011. As a country, despite our relatively high uptake by international comparisons, we have fallen short of the WHO aims. The UK current target for flu vaccine uptake is 75% for people aged 65 years and over as recommended by the WHO; and 75% uptake for people under age 65 with clinical conditions which put them more at risk from the effects of flu.

Some immunisations are even more contentious. Since September 2008 there has been a national programme to vaccinate girls aged 12 to 13 and to catch up with older girls aged 14 to 17, against the human papilloma virus (HPV), also known as the cervical cancer jab. The programme is delivered in secondary schools and consists of three injections that should ideally be given over a period of six months, although they can all be given over a period of 12 months.

Case study: The HPV vaccination

Mrs Foster, the wife of a patient on the surgical ward, asks a nurse for advice. She wants to know whether to allow her 14-year-old daughter to have the HPV vaccination. The nurse is interested to know why Mrs Foster is questioning this as in her view the daughter should have all the protection she can get against cervical cancer.

The nurse sits down with Mrs Foster and asks her to say why she thinks the vaccination should not proceed. Mrs Foster says that she knows it's about a sexually transmitted disease and her daughter doesn't have sex. She fears the immunisation will make her daughter think about having sex when she is too young. Mrs Foster feels the school should not be allowing the issue of sex to be raised.

The nurse asks whether Mrs Foster has agreed to her daughter attending sex education classes at the school. She discovers that Mrs Foster has not withdrawn her daughter from classes (although she is entitled to), she has just allowed them to continue. The nurse continues to discuss the overall approach the school seems to have to sex education and states that in her professional opinion knowledge and understanding about sex is more likely to prevent early sexual experimentation than to encourage it. The nurse suggests that the HPV

continued opposite...

continued... ••••••••••••••••••••••••

immunisation would raise further awareness of risks of sexual intercourse and may deter her daughter from trying sex.

She goes on to explain that having the vaccination before sexual activity begins is more effective and it is the government's intention to create a general level of immunity in girls and young women. Mrs Foster agrees that it does, after all, seem a good idea and is pleased when the nurse gives her the website address for NHS Choices (**www.nhs.uk**) on which she can look up the HPV vaccine.

The role of health professionals in helping people to decide about immunisations is partly to allay fears which circulate in horror stories and rumour. We learned the lesson well from the problems caused by poor research into MMR vaccine (a combination vaccine for measles, mumps and rubella). Because of misleading research findings people became afraid of the effects of MMR, the uptake was poor and the result was low herd immunity resulting in several outbreaks of the diseases. Measles in particular is a disease which can kill, and children died in the outbreaks. Mumps in adults is more serious than in children (causing more severe symptoms and taking longer to recover). The effect of not vaccinating with MMR for several years was when those unvaccinated children became adults at 18 and went to college and university, leaving home to live in community residences, outbreaks of mumps occurred in these places. As a nurse your opinion is respected by the public and it is important that you find out the facts and the best advice to give. MMR is safe and immunisation prevents communicable diseases; that is the message we should be giving the public.

Having looked at a major part of what constitutes public health – communicable diseases – we will now return to an aspect of disease surveillance which appeared earlier but which was not explored. In explaining what public health is we mentioned that the current white paper (DH, 2010a) includes 'tackling the wider determinants of ill health' and later in Activity 6.2 we asked you to look out for any differences in disease distribution due to 'social classes or income levels'. These allude to the issue of who is at more risk from ill health due to social rather than physical factors.

Inequalities in health

Concept summary: Health inequalities

Since the Black Report in 1974 it has been known that social class impacts on health. Low socio-economic status (and particularly poverty) leads to a disproportionately high level of ill health. This was confirmed by Whitehead's work of 1988. Ignored or denied by the Conservatives, the issue was highlighted by the Labour government between 1998 and 2010. They commissioned the Acheson Report in 1998, which re-emphasised the fact that poverty and other social disadvantages affect health.

The current work on inequalities in health is informed by the Marmot (2010) review, which sets out six policy objectives:

continued overleaf...

continued...

- give every child the best start in life;
- enable all children, young people and adults to maximise their capabilities and have control over their lives;
- create fair employment and good work for all;
- ensure a healthy standard of living for all;
- create and develop healthy and sustainable places and communities;
- strengthen the role and impact of ill health prevention.

The history of the UK acknowledging and working on health inequalities originates in 1974 with the Black Report and shows how long the struggle has been to resolve these problems. Inequalities in health are still a major government agenda today. The health of individuals and communities is greatly affected by social and environmental circumstances; the UK has poverty, poor housing, poor education, poor employment and social disadvantage today and public health continues to try to reduce these inequalities.

Working in partnership with other sectors such as housing, education and employment, public health and other health professionals seek to improve those social, economic and environmental circumstances which can trap people into cycles of disadvantage and therefore ill health. Improving health is not only about physical prevention such as immunisation, and not only about educating people about health: people need to be in better circumstances to have better chances of health.

Case study: What caused the accident?

Kenny Townsend is a 25-year-old man who has had an accident on his residential street, tripping and injuring his leg and shoulder badly while trying to stop his little boy running into the road. His physical condition has been directly caused by the accident – but what caused the accident?

Kenny is unemployed, so he spends a lot of time walking the streets as he cannot find a job. He cannot find a job because he did not finish school – he went to a school which had poor standards and he did not attend very much. He has low levels of reading and other work skills, and he has not managed to keep a job for long.

Kenny does not have much money. He and his partner live in a council flat on the estate and have two children. Most of the money goes on household bills so Kenny's shoes are very cheap and not sturdy. Because of the money situation, Kenny tends to spend what he has for himself on drinking with his friends most days.

The estate where Kenny and Susie live is run down, the roads and pavements are poorly maintained and there are many cars and vans and bicycles on the move constantly. There are no buses, so people have to own a vehicle or walk to the main road to get to the town centre. There are no play facilities for children on the estate.

Both Kenny and Susie's parents live on the estate too. Their fathers are also long-term unemployed and had poor schooling. Susie and her mother were teenage mothers and neither has ever been employed.

What then caused the accident?

Consider the case study about Kenny's accident. The family background is one of poor education, poor housing and low income, all resulting in poor health chances. The shoes, the alcohol, the road, the lack of learning, the lack of good child facilities, and the lack of money all contributed to the accident. Educating Kenny about accident prevention is only a small part of the solution. Can you see now how social, economic and environmental factors affect health?

Chapter summary

This chapter has explored the meaning of public health and the nurse's role in the wider aspects of public health. You should now have a better understanding of the function of public health organisations and professionals. There has been a focus on communicable diseases in order to explain and help you understand your role, which is not what nurses think of everyday as a nursing role. Inequalities in health have been introduced in order to help you envisage the whole picture of what causes ill health. As you continue to care for patients, you can consider the social, economic and environmental factors which brought them into your care.

Activities: Brief outline answers

Activity 6.4 (page 96)

The vaccine may cause Mr Watkins to feel a bit off-colour for a day but will not cause him to develop flu. While his immune system reacts to the vaccine his temperature may go up a little and he may feel sleepy and not want to eat because of this. The injection site may be very slightly inflamed. Any symptoms worse than this must be reported to his doctor, as he may have developed another infection while trying to respond to the vaccine.

He needs to know that it is better to be protected than to risk getting flu, which can be a severe illness, and may kill vulnerable people. The vaccine offered each year is the best available for the predicted outbreak that year.

Finally, tell him that if he has any fever or infection at the time of the appointment he must cancel or tell the nurse when he gets there. The immunisation should not be done when his immune system is fighting another infection, as he could become more ill – but he still would not get flu.

In addition, you must make sure that Mr Watkins is not immune-deficient because of cancer chemotherapy, organ transplant or HIV infection. This would mean that he only gets the flu vaccine under the care of his specialist experts.

Further reading

Department of Health (2010) *Our Health and Wellbeing Today*. London: DH.
This is the accompanying document to the current public health white paper for England. It contains a lot of information about health issues in the country, including statistics.

Coles, L and Porter, E (eds) (2009) *Public Health Skills: a practical guide for nurses and public health practitioners*. Oxford: Blackwell Publishing.
An edited book with chapter writers explaining a comprehensive range of skills for improving health in communities.

Useful websites

www.dh.gov.uk/en/Publichealth/index.htm
The public health section of the Department of Health website. News will be on the front page, and recent documents are easily accessible. Use their search box to look up your topic.

www.hpa.org.uk/
Website of the Health Protection Agency. News of the latest outbreaks and incidents will be on the front page.

www.apho.org.uk/
The Association of Public Health Observatories represents a network of 12 public health observatories working across the five nations of England, Scotland, Wales, Northern Ireland and the Republic of Ireland. They produce information, data and intelligence on people's health and health care for practitioners, policy makers and the wider community.

www.statistics.gov.uk/hub/health-social-care/index.html
The government's website for all UK health statistics.

Chapter 7
Managing health promotion in practice

NMC Standards for Pre-registration Nursing Education

This chapter will address the following competencies:

Domain 1: Professional values

5. All nurses must fully understand the nurse's various roles, responsibilities and functions, and adapt practice to meet the changing needs of people, groups, communities and populations.

Domain 4: Leadership, management and team working

7. All nurses must work effectively across professional and agency boundaries, actively involving and respecting others' contributions to integrated person-centered care. They must know when and how to communicate with and refer to other professionals and agencies in order to respect the choices of service users and others, promoting shared decision-making, to deliver positive outcomes and to coordinate smooth, effective transition within and between services and agencies.

NMC Essential Skills Clusters

This chapter will address the following ESCs:

Cluster: Organisational aspects of care

14. People can trust the newly registered graduate nurse to be an autonomous and confident member of the multi-disciplinary or multi-agency team and to inspire confidence in others.

By the second progression point:

3. Values others' roles and responsibilities within the team and interacts appropriately.

By entry to the register:

6. Actively consults and explores solutions and ideas with others to enhance care.
7. Challenges the practice of self and others across the multi-professional team.
8. Takes an effective role within the team adopting the leadership role when appropriate.
9. Acts as an effective role model in decision-making, taking action and supporting others.
10. Works inter-professionally and autonomously as a means of achieving optimum outcomes for people.

> ### Chapter aims
>
> By the end of the chapter you will be able to:
>
> - discuss the concept of settings-based health promotion;
> - identify skills for health promotion practice;
> - discuss the planning, implementation and evaluation process for a health promotion activity;
> - appreciate the wide range of possible partners in health promotion practice.

Introduction

In the twenty-first century, you, as a health promoter, need to develop a health promotion practice which embraces the broader context of health which includes the physical, psychological, socio-economic and environmental dimensions of wellbeing as discussed in Chapters 1 and 6.

In order to manage this practice, you, as a health promoter, need to adopt a systematic and structured approach to health promotion which expands beyond NHS boundaries. You have to develop health promotion activity which does not focus exclusively on your patients in a hospital setting but you need to consider how you are going to promote wellbeing which is sustainable within their own environment in the community.

This chapter will explore where and how health promotion can be planned, and who can work together with nurses. It will look at the skills nurses need to plan and manage quality health promotion in hospital and with communities.

Understanding healthy settings in the context of your nursing practice

The WHO advocates that health promotion must take place within different settings which are referred to as 'healthy settings', namely healthy schools, healthy universities, healthy hospitals, healthy workplaces and healthy neighbourhoods, to mention a few. The overarching aim is to target the whole population at the different stages of their life span, for example children in schools, adults in their workplaces and everyone including older people in their neighbourhoods.

Nurses can work in a variety of such settings to promote well-being and positive health

Concept summary: Health promotion settings for nurses

- NHS: NHS hospital trusts (adult nurses, mental health, children's nurses);
- NHS: local community health organisations (practice nurses, health visitors, district nurses, psychiatric community nurses and community nurses for learning disabilities);

continued opposite...

continued...

- local authority: education: schools, colleges, universities (school nurses, occupational health nurses);
- local authority: social care: residential homes, sheltered accommodation and nursing homes (adult nurses, mental health nurses, nurses for learning disabilities);
- local authority with voluntary sector: neighbourhoods, housing estates, town centres, community centres, faith centres (health visitors, community nurses, nurses from all branches depending on speciality);
- private sector: private hospitals, workplaces such as car manufacturing and department stores (occupational health nurses, nurses from all branches depending on speciality);
- prisons (adult nurses, mental health nurses).

Settings such as these give nurses opportunities to develop health promotion activities suitable to the whole setting, not just to a particular target group on a particular health topic. Any one setting can include health promotion for everyone who is there (workers, visitors, students, patients, local families), on a range of topics such as coronary heart disease and cancers prevention, smoking, healthy eating, accident prevention and so on, whatever seems most relevant. This is a different approach to targeting groups and topics singly – for example a teenage pregnancy project.

A setting is not only determined by its geography and the sector which finances the service provision. The WHO (WHO, 1998b) views a setting as the place in which people engage in daily activities such as working, learning, playing and loving. As a nurse you can identify with this concept of a setting, as it echoes the principles of the activities of daily living, which provides a familiar framework for your nursing practice. Alongside the daily activities you need to consider the setting's physical environment and infrastructure as well as people's personal factors, which interact to create and affect health and wellbeing. This means that you, as health promoter, have to view people (including your patients) as part of their socio-economic context in which they live and to consider how this impacts upon their health (Chapter 6). You will need to work out very carefully which framework of health promotion practice will be most appropriate for the setting in which you are going to deliver your health promotion interventions, for example you may use a social change approach or an empowerment approach (see Chapter 1).

Therefore from the health promotion perspective it seems highly appropriate that the concept of healthy settings is widely used by different governments in their health policies to promote health:

- by solving health-related problems closer to their source;
- by recognising that the social, physical and economic environments form an integral part of people's health.

Today the healthy settings approach in health promotion practice has been built on a number of the WHO's Charters and Declarations (see Chapter 1), namely the Ottawa Charter (WHO, 1986), Sundsvall (WHO, 1991), Jakarta Declaration (WHO, 1997) and Bangkok charter (WHO, 2005). All of them act as catalysts in adopting the settings approach as the way forward for health promotion practice. They highlight the importance of settings in the development and implementation of comprehensive health promotion strategies to improve people's health status and quality of life. They stress that promotion of health and wellbeing requires the creation of supportive environments which include not only healthcare settings but also places such as home, work and recreational facilities. They urge individual governments to invest in the provision of a settings infrastructure to promote health. In the UK this has materialised in the format of healthy hospitals, healthy universities, healthy schools, healthy workplaces, and healthy neighbourhoods.

Healthy Cities (WHO, 1978) provided the blueprint for the implementation of the healthy settings approach to achieve health gain. The healthy cities programme uses health promotion interventions based on a social model responding to people's health needs as perceived and determined by them (felt, expressed and comparative) rather than on the 'normative' health needs determined by the professionals. It focuses on priorities for change as determined by the people and acknowledges that people's behaviour is shaped by the structural factors of their living environment.

However, you, as a health promoter, have to be aware that there are substantial differences between the different settings in relation to their organisational structure, ideological ethos as presented in the mission statements, culture, and size, for example a hospital has a formal and hierarchical institutional culture in comparison to a residential care setting, which could be informal and more linear in structure. You need also to be aware that there are differences between the social contexts of settings belonging to the same sector, for example a school in an inner city has an inherently different social context to a school in a rural area.

These differences and the complexities of the setting within which people live their lives are very important, and you need to bear them in mind when you plan and deliver health promotion interventions. Your health promotion activities have to be relevant and tailor-made for your target group.

Case study: The varying needs and cultures of different target groups

Nurse Ryan is a family planning nurse. She has been invited to deliver a session on sex education in two local comprehensive schools. The two schools have different social environments. School A is located in the poorest part of the local area while school B is situated in the most affluent part of the locality.

Nurse Ryan prepared the same content for both sessions. On the day of delivering the session she used a student-centred approach. Both sessions were very interactive and she felt that the students gained a lot from the session. However, she noticed that students' discussions in the two schools were differently focused. The students in the two schools were interested in different things.

School A students wanted to know more about fertility, as they were keen to have babies and they had very romantic views of having intimate relationships. Many young girls perceived motherhood as the way forward as they were not too keen to continue with their education.

School B students were very keen to know about contraception, effectiveness and provision of contraceptive services. They were ambitious and wanted to further advance their education.

Both sets of students, though, were asking similar questions, for example regarding confidentiality issues and availability of young people's clinics in their area.

This case study highlights that nurses have to adjust their practice to meet the needs of their target group and culture of the setting.

A settings approach challenges nurses to take the lead to improve the health status of the whole population rather than people who are ill. You have to develop skills in managing health promotion practice and to establish networking as well as to form partnerships (Chapter 1). This means that you as a health promoter need to expand the horizon of your activities and to reconsider the nature of your practice, both of which will be discussed in the following sections.

Health promotion practice within an NHS setting: hospital and community

NHS Hospital Trusts and **NHS local community health services** are in a strong position, as settings, to provide health promotion, as they have professional expertise and captive target groups (staff, patients and visitors). Staff are generally well respected and valued by the public and therefore they are seen as credible sources for health information and consultation.

Currently the majority of nurses working within an NHS setting are involved with health promotion activities focusing on solving health problems, as presented by individual patients, and therefore the focus of their health promotion is orientated around disease prevention and management of disease. The activity constitutes part of the care plan documentation and is mainly delivered in the format of tertiary prevention (treatment and rehabilitation), health advice (Chapters 1 and 4) and behaviour change (Chapter 2).

One may argue that tertiary prevention is more typical of the health promotion work of nurses working within the hospital setting, than of nurses working in the primary care setting. Nurses in primary care have a wider scope of health promotion activity than the hospital nurses as they are engaged for example in primary prevention, i.e. vaccination and immunisation programmes, secondary prevention, i.e. screening, health checks and travel health services. However, health advice and behaviour change is needed in both sections of the NHS.

Nurses in NHS healthcare settings encounter many competing factors which constrain health promotion activities, for example clinical and care management issues, staffing levels, work load. As a result, health promotion is very often unplanned and opportunistic in nature, which can be effective, but more could be achieved if health promotion is integrated within the organisation and delivery of care.

Whether a hospital or community care area is committed to improving and maintaining good health promotion practice depends to a large extent on the vision and skills of its senior nurses. You may see areas which are doing some of the following, for example:

* planning calendar health events such as breast awareness month, no smoking day, HIV/AIDS and sexual health week etc. – health events aim to encourage people to stay healthy as well as to change behaviour;
* making available health promotion leaflets relating to health topics of their specialty as a resource accessible to staff, visitors and patients;

- ensuring that every patient receives a health education programme which is standardised and recorded within the nursing care 'package';
- designating one qualified nurse as 'health promotion nurse' for the area, to coordinate activities and keep everyone else aware of the need.

As a qualified nurse you will need to become a catalyst for change by promoting and developing a practice within the NHS which is driven by national and international health strategies. If the organisation you work for does not have a strong and sustainable health promotion practice, be bold enough to suggest how they can improve. Start small in a small area or with one topic and care group, but go ahead and try something!

However, it has to be acknowledged that this can only be achieved by you developing competencies and skills to undertake the management of health promotion projects, by becoming a self-confident, knowledgeable practitioner with special expertise in health promotion, a political player and an active as well as influential participant in decision-making at the organisational level. At present nurses are seen as 'doers' at the grass roots (micro) level rather than as initiators of change and active participants in the decision-making at a higher organisational (macro) level. As a graduate nurse, you will need to assert yourself in a leadership position regarding health promotion practice and to possess negotiation skills in order to gain the organisation's management support for funding, and to develop collaborative action. Planning, implementation and evaluation have to be the steering forces of managing health promotion practice at micro or macro level.

Managing health promotion practice in any setting requires a wide range of skills. Some of them are transferable skills from your nursing practice, as for example interprofessional working, communication, planning, implementing and evaluating practice, as you will find out by doing Activity 7.1.

Activity 7.1   *Critical thinking and reflection*

You are working in a GP surgery as part of your clinical experience. The local community health organisation for the surgery in collaboration with the local hospital, which has been awarded a healthy hospital status, have gained funding to develop a three-year programme with the aim of improving the quality of life of people who suffer with mental health problems in their local area. Your designated mentor Theresa has been given the remit to develop this programme. Theresa decides that the target group will be unemployed people who are known to be at risk of mental health problems. Theresa's objectives are:

- to set up a support group to enable them to come to terms and cope with their personal problems;
- to establish a drop-in centre which is easily accessible.

When Theresa discussed with you the proposed development, you expressed interest and volunteered to shadow Theresa during the developmental process of the programme. Now make a list of the skills which you think Theresa will use during the planning process.

A brief outline answer for this activity is provided at the end of the chapter.

Reflecting on the activity, you may have identified a number of transferable skills from your nursing practice or your previous experiences; however, you may have encountered some difficulty in translating them into health promotion practice suitable to the setting, as well as with your role as an enabler, mediator and advocate of patients.

The organisation Skills for Health was tasked with generating a list of skills for public health at specialist and practitioner levels in 2004. Specialists are professionals who are in charge of public health locally and nationally, who act to manage public health locally and control emergencies (see Chapter 6). Public health practitioners can be from a variety of professions whose job includes working on improving health. This includes nurses on the NMC public health part of the register (see Chapter 6). You can use this list here to think about your own development of skills in the context of managing health promotion in practice, some skills will not be essential until you are the person in charge. You may like to refer back to this section when you have read Chapter 8 about keeping up your skills.

Concept summary: Skills and competencies for health promotion practice (Skills for Health 2004) summarised and interpreted for you as students of nursing

Area 1: Surveillance and assessment of the population's health and wellbeing

Being able to understand how health data is collected, interpreted and used to assess health needs of people and communities.

Area 2: Promoting and protecting the population's health and wellbeing

Learning how to provide health information to people and communities, helping them to change to healthy behaviour. Observing work in partnership with others to plan, implement, monitor and evaluate health promotion initiatives.

Area 3: Developing quality and risk management within an evaluative culture

Seeing senior professionals managing others to attain good standards of health promotion.

Area 4: Collaborative working for health and wellbeing

Appreciating that working in partnership with people and organisations to set up health promotion (interprofessional, interagency and intersectoral) is complex and can be effective.

Area 5: Developing health programmes and services and reducing inequalities

Beginning to organise resources and funding for health promotion activities suitable for addressing health needs. Understanding methods of addressing inequalities in health.

Area 6: Policy and strategy development and implementation to improve health and wellbeing

Reading and understanding health policies and strategies to improve health. Analysing the policy decisions.

continued overleaf...

continued...

Area 7: Working with and for communities to improve health and wellbeing

Studying the literature and making observations about how health promotion projects can enable development of skills in individuals and the community.

Area 8: Strategic leadership for health and wellbeing

Observing the leadership of others in managing health promotion.

Area 9: Research and development to improve health and wellbeing

Learning to read and understand research literature, and then to implement findings.

Area 10: Ethically managing self, people and resources to improve health and wellbeing

Continue to develop management skills generally.

Some of the skills summarised are generic and you may already have used them during your nursing practice; the idea is that you can see what you need to develop to become a good health promoting nurse. Chapter 8 will remind you again of the NHS Knowledge and Skills Framework (KSF) created in 2004. In the KSF Health and Wellbeing dimension the same skills are expressed in terms of required achievement for NHS employees, and will be used to appraise your performance as a qualified nurse.

As with your nursing practice you need to consider how you are going to find evidence of good practice in health promotion, which will inform your own practice and can be replicated to your setting. For example, imagine you are planning to implement the National Service Framework for Diabetes to promote healthy drinking for your diabetic patients. You need to do a literature review to establish effectiveness of similar projects and to review how others have set up the projects. You may also need to use epidemiological evidence to support and justify the need for such a project in your setting. Good IT skills and knowing how to conduct literature search skills are crucial. Use different search engines as sources, i.e. MEDLINE, Cochrane database of systematic reviews, DARE (Database of reviews of effectiveness) and the EPPI Centre (Register of reviews of effectiveness in health promotion).

Once you have read the gathered literature you need to critically analyse the material and to consider selection of health promotion interventions appropriate for your own setting. Many students find it difficult to analyse read material (literature). An easy way to achieve this is by considering yourself to be a good detective. Be inquisitive and always ask yourself: What does this mean for my practice? What are the implications for my practice? You need to translate the meaning of what you have read and to make judgement of read material in relation to quality, relevance, applicability and implications for your practice.

Identification of health needs enables you to set health promotion priorities, encourages patients' participation and promotes a health promotion practice which is patient-centred; therefore it is pertinent that you understand the hierarchy of needs. Bradshaw's taxonomy of need (Bradshaw, 1972) gives you a useful classification of need which can guide your practice.

Concept summary: Bradshaw's taxonomy of need

1. Normative needs

These are determined by professionals; for example you as a nurse made the decision that diabetic patients need to have health education on foot care. The needs represent your professional judgement and do not represent your patients' wishes. This is a top-down approach and does not take into account your patients' personal circumstances or factors which may interact with their diabetes and affect their overall health and wellbeing. Health promotion takes the form of information giving and it very often reduces patients' concordance.

2. Felt needs

These are what your patients actually want. In the case of your diabetic patients they may want better services and easier access to chiropodists. This allows for a bottom-up approach and you may act as a mediator to improve chiropodist service in the setting. However, you need to be aware that felt needs are based on individual perceptions and your patients may not actually be aware of the available chiropodist service in the locality, in which case you then provide information regarding access and availability of services.

3. Expressed needs

These are 'felt' needs turned into action and therefore have become a demand. Your diabetic patients are complaining about the prolonged waiting times to see a chiropodist in their locality. You need to be cautious that quite often the expressed needs represent the patients who are articulate and have the power and ability to make their voices heard. There is a danger that the most 'needy' may not express their needs and therefore health inequalities persist.

4. Comparative needs

These occur when a group of diabetic patients does not receive any health promotion activity in relation to foot care while another group which is similar in characteristics and of a similar setting receives health promotion regarding diabetic foot care. This has been highlighted in relation to the so-called postcode lottery when patients, depending where they live, may or may not have access to certain treatment, for example NHS fertility treatment.

A skilful assessment, clear understanding and correct interpretation of health needs enables you, as health promoter, to set health priorities which represent the actual health needs of the setting's population and you can plan appropriate and relevant interventions which will determine successful and positive outcomes of practice. You need to be aware that normative needs inform most of health promotion activity in an NHS hospital ward or local community health setting while felt and expressed needs will often be the guiding force on community development, which is usually operated in partnership with the community.

You need to be skilful in identifying the views of the stakeholders. They are the people in the setting who have vested interest in the health promotion project (i.e. managers, budget holders) and they want to influence the 'what and how' of your health promotion practice. You need to pay attention to their views as they are in a position of power. However, you will need to establish that they do not comprise the calibre and overall purpose of your practice. This is very difficult to achieve and requires very skilful negotiation.

You need also to consider your target group who are the recipients of the project. You need to pay attention to their values, beliefs, behaviour pattern, customs and culture, aspirations and attitudes. Your practice has to consider all these elements in order to be accepted by your target group.

This means paying attention to conflicts of interest between stakeholders and target group and how these impending tensions may affect your practice within the setting. You need to be confident, assertive, to have self-esteem and be an effective communicator and counsellor.

You need to develop clear understanding of underpinning communication theories and to evaluate their merits (Chapters 2 and 4). This will enable you to use a range of approaches to support people and facilitate change by promoting health-enhancing relationships which increase self-esteem and improve self-concept (Chapters 1 and 2). By using the right language and by demonstrating understanding of their individual setting, you will be able to gain their cooperation. They will be motivated to engage in decision-making. They will feel comfortable to seek support when they encounter difficulties.

The success of your practice depends on your management skills: you will need to employ a variety of management skills in order to develop a health promotion practice.

- You will need to be able to manage change, for example from what is done currently, which may be unplanned and under-resourced, to a formal, structured and well-organised practice.
- You have to be diplomatic, involve your colleagues in the decision-making process, gain their cooperation and be careful not to alienate them!
- Team building skills are crucial, as coordination and team work are vital. Health promotion practice involves working with people from different sectors and different departments. Therefore it is vital to promote team building to maintain good relationships.
- Time management skills are very important and very difficult to achieve as you may have already experienced while studying in the nursing degree course. As a nurse working in a very busy setting you are involved with a wide range of work roles, all of which compete for your time. You need to devise a realistic work schedule and ensure adherence to the schedule.
- You will need to seek management support, their approval and secure their commitment to your practice. Negotiation skills will be helpful here.
- You will select a wide spectrum of resources for your practice (human and material). Critical review of various resources is an important element. You have to develop expertise in establishing their effectiveness, appropriateness and accessibility. You have to ask such questions as: Do they use clear language suitable for my target group? Are they non-racist, non-sexist? Are there any legal issues regarding consent? What is the evidence of their effectiveness? Who is the author(s)? What are his/her qualifications and expertise on the

subject matter? Do they promote the interest of any particular party? See Chapter 4 for more details on choosing resources.

- Your role as health promoter also requires you to become an active networker and effective collaborator. High quality collaborative action and skilful networking can be instrumental to successful, effective and efficient health promotion practice. This requires development of organisational, social, political, interpersonal, negotiation and leadership skills. In an NHS setting nurses as patients' advocates, mediators and enablers have to take the lead in forming partnerships (see Chapter 1). The partnership has to incorporate professionals drawn from the broad spectrum of the setting's multidisciplinary team, i.e. doctors, physiotherapists, managers, specialist nurses, social workers and health promotion specialists as well as external agents, i.e. pharmaceutical companies.
- Your health promotion practice in an NHS setting will involve the development of a project or a programme, which is informed by national health policies and as such they are funded by central government. However, very often you may be involved with local initiatives and as such you have to raise additional funds from other sources, for example the national lottery. Thus you need to develop skills in writing proposals and presentation skills to secure funding for project/activity, and the ability to use spreadsheets to estimate and monitor costs.

As a nurse already, you have the acquisition of planning, implementing and evaluating skills through the nursing process and will be able to transfer them to health promotion practice.

You need to assert your health promotion role by re-addressing your scope of practice from an opportunistic, unplanned mode of practice to a well-thought scheduled practice underpinned by the theoretical principles of planning, implemention and evaluation. Health promotion is frequently criticised for its lack of evaluation. Nowadays, working in an economic climate of austerity, you need to provide evidence not only of an effective and efficient practice but of a health promotion practice which has an economic, social and health impact. This can be achieved by the process of evaluation.

Activity 7.2   *Critical thinking*

As a graduate nurse, you are the designated nurse for health promotion in an acute medical ward. The ward manager during a ward meeting reported that according to the admissions statistics there was a marked increase of hospital admissions due to testicular cancer. During the meeting it was agreed that you should organise a health event in the main part of the hospital to promote awareness of testicular cancer among staff, patients and visitors.

- Now think how you will plan, implement and evaluate the 'event'.

An outline answer is given at the end of this chapter.

Chapter 1 offers some theoretical frameworks, for example Tannahill's (1986) model of health promotion, which help you to understand the nature and intention of health promotion practice. They also enable you to select and use appropriate interventions to improve the health of your patients; in Tannahill's model, education, prevention and policy. However, they do not give you a clear direction on the 'know how' to structure and manage your practice. Project planning processes are helpful here. These consist of different well-defined stages which echo the nursing process, that is, the planning, setting goals, implementing and evaluating process. The process provides you with a series of linear stages which relate to each other and are cyclical in nature. They are very easy to follow and by the application of relevant skills, as discussed in this section, enable you to organise and manage your health promotion practice.

Concept summary: Project planning process

1. Assess needs and priorities.
2. Set aims and objectives.
3. Decide the best way of achieving the aims and objectives.
4. Identify resources.
5. Plan evaluation methods.
6. Set an action plan with details, dates and who does what.
7. Action! Implement your plan, including your evaluation.
8. Compile a report for the organisation and for your portfolio.

The stages provide a framework for practice which is already familiar to you and forms an integral part of your organisation of nursing care. They effectively enable you to incorporate health promotion as part of your nursing practice. This process can be applied to individual patient care also, and therefore the 'patient teaching process' can run parallel to the nursing process in operation. As a means of planning an independent project, however, it is a systematic approach to work and as such will be helpful to you whenever you want to introduce some new initiative into your practice.

Case study: Project planning

Raj is an occupational health nurse in a large manufacturing company and he wants to start an awareness-raising initiative about high blood pressure. He has thought of this after noticing the increasing number of workers who have told him they are on medication for the condition (1). Raj thinks he needs to see that all the workers understand about high blood pressure and that they all have regular screening tests whether they are hypertensive or not (2). He feels he can do this by displaying information throughout the workplace, attaching leaflets to all the payslips and setting times to do the screening, inviting all the different departments to sessions (3). He will need posters, leaflets, permission from management and cooperation from the wages department. He decides to get his equipment checked and updated, and to design a card for each worker in which to record the blood pressure readings and advice given (4). Raj then plans to evaluate by firstly asking all staff to complete a short questionnaire about their understanding of hypertension and its effects; he then plans to use the same questionnaire in six months' time to see the differences. He will also keep confidential records of the screenings to see whether people are taking notice of his advice and whether there are any changes in how the hypertensive people are keeping control (5). Raj sets out a timetable for action over the first six months, with a view to continue the programme if it is successful (6).

Hopefully Raj's initiative will show some good results and he can write a report (8) for management who may consider providing more resources for his next innovation. In this case the occupational health

continued opposite...

continued...

nurse worked virtually alone and this is part of the nature of the job. You may find you can organise small initiatives in this way with the help of managers, resources providers and others who can provide some practical support. However, a principle of wider health promotion practice is that of working in partnership.

Partnership working: interprofessional, interagency and intersectoral

Nurses are not the only people who do health promotion as part of their role. Other health professionals all have the responsibility to teach patients and to contribute to health promotion initiatives. You will find that the hospital-based health professionals tend to concentrate on teaching patients as hospital nurses do, and community professionals tend to be the ones to work on wider projects.

The term agency refers to the different organisations that exist in all aspects of the community. The GP practice and the sexual health clinic working together are two agencies within the NHS. The specialist colo-rectal nurse working with the charity Beating Bowel Cancer are also two agencies, this time across two sectors; public (NHS) and voluntary (charity). Different health professionals, different agencies and different sectors working together will all have their primary functions and unilateral ways of doing things. The primary function of a catering company is to sell food, so will they agree to your healthy eating advice in your project? The potential breadth of partners across professions, agencies and sectors can be large and at times clumsy. The various power levels of partners can get in the way of joint working. When partnership is effective, however, it can form a useful range of expertise and resources, and can be a powerful force for change. Activity 7.3 asks you to consider this breadth and will make you think about the skills you will need to communicate, network and manage a team.

Activity 7.3   *Team working*

You are working in the community with a district nurse who has decided to set up an awareness-raising event in the local community centre. The event will target elderly South Asian people and the topic is diabetes type 2 (non-insulin-dependent).

At an informal meeting with the local specialist diabetes care nurse, the district nurse asks you to contribute to a brainstorm on who can be involved in this event – what ideas can you think of across the health professions, agencies and sectors?

An outline answer is given at the end of this chapter.

From this activity you can see the possible range of help available through working in partnership to do health promotion. It is a time-consuming and complex way to work, but an enriching experience essential to a settings-based approach.

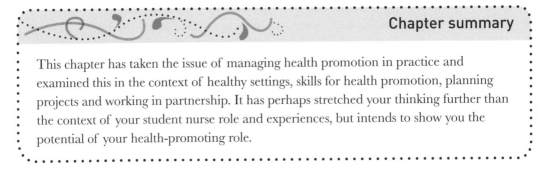

Chapter summary

This chapter has taken the issue of managing health promotion in practice and examined this in the context of healthy settings, skills for health promotion, planning projects and working in partnership. It has perhaps stretched your thinking further than the context of your student nurse role and experiences, but intends to show you the potential of your health-promoting role.

Activities: Brief outline answers

Activity 7.1 (page 106)

Theresa will use a range of skills as specified by Skills for Health (2004).

*   Collection of epidemiological data to ascertain the scale of the problem, i.e. how many unemployed people live in the area and what are the rates of mental health problems among unemployed people?
*   Communicate with the unemployed and some key health professionals about the project and assess health needs.
*   Do a literature search for evidence and examples of best practice.
*   Understand local policies on mental health and know the local facilities.
*   Assess resources required for the project and secure funding.
*   Set up a team or teams; identify and manage interprofessional working.
*   Organise a work schedule.
*   Lead the work of teams to achieve the project's objectives.

You may have noted other skills which occur to you, such as the transferable skills of communication, IT skills, teamwork, or things like writing skills and planning skills. The idea is that many skills are needed for this complex task.

Activity 7.2 (page 111)

You will need to create a time schedule, i.e. time for event preparation, fix date of event, evaluation of event, writing up and publication.

*   Form partnerships with other professionals who can contribute and participate in the organisation of the event (internal and external to the hospital), organise meetings, agree tasks, divide up the work, arrange staffing for the event.
*   Set and agree aims and objectives for the event.
*   Contact UK cancer and men's health organisations for current health information and promotion material such as posters, leaflets, DVDs, models and illustrations of the body parts, quizzes on the facts.
*   Order and review the resources; organise the venue and think about layout of the display.
*   Complete a health and safety risk assessment regarding venue and event.
*   Discuss how you are going to approach the public and engage them in conversation.
*   Design the event advertising and market the event. Remember you need to invite visitors, patients and staff.
*   Plan the day; start and finish times, who will set up and clear away. Organise tasks for each helper and a work schedule including coffee breaks.

- Keep a record of how many people came to the event, how many leaflets they took, how many participants completed quizzes. Ask people to write down what they think of the event.
- Arrange debriefing meeting with partners and ascertain how they felt the day went.

Write an evaluative report of the event and publish internally or externally.

Make an entry in your professional portfolio.

Activity 7.3 (page 113)

You may have other ideas – but here are a few potential partners as well as the district nurse and the diabetes specialist nurse:

Community dietician, community podiatrist, community physiotherapist, local GP practice nurse. Is there an advanced nurse practitioner in diabetes? Local health promotion department in the community health organisation (PCT).

Local group of Diabetes UK. The national organisation can be contacted for help too.

Some volunteer members of the South Asian community (patients?), Asian Women's Association. Faith leaders – Moslem, Hindu, Sikh, Buddhist, Catholic.

Local Asian shopkeepers and the trade association. Local supermarket, or street market traders.

Some food manufacturers (ask the advice of the community dietician) – for example wholemeal bread and sugar-free smoothies.

Drug and equipment (blood sugar monitors, pharmaceutical companies) suppliers – but only those who are on the local NHS supplies contract list.

Further reading

Verzuh, E (1999) *The Fast Forward MBA in Project Management.* Chichester: Wiley.
A very comprehensive and detailed guide to managing projects in any area. It has many ideas for organising effective teams and achieving outcomes.

Coles, L and Porter, E (eds) (2009) *Public Health Skills: a practical guide for nurses and public health practitioners.* Oxford: Blackwell Publishing.
An edited book with chapter writers explaining a comprehensive range of skills for improving health in communities.

Goodman, B and Clemow, R (2010) *Nursing and Collaborative Practice.* Exeter: Learning Matters.
A good book on working together and team work.

Useful websites

www.who.int/healthy_settings/en/
The WHO's site for healthy settings of all kinds across the world.

www.uclan.ac.uk/schools/school_of_health/research_projects/hsdu/healthy_settings_development_unit.php
The UK Healthy Settings Development Unit, based at the University of Central Lancashire. The place to find out what settings are used here, and the news about them.

Chapter 8
Keeping up your skills

Introduction

This chapter focuses on keeping up your skills for health-promoting nursing practice. It considers the importance of understanding the guidance from the NMC with regard to continuing professional development. There are a variety of ways you may wish to keep up to date in health promotion practice and some suggestions are presented. It is also important to consider how you will collect the evidence of this work that you have undertaken; this will be needed to underpin your professional practice.

Developing health-promoting practice skills

Developing the skills of being an effective health-promoting nurse in your workplace is a demanding but satisfactory area of your practice. The best way to become a health-promoting nurse is not to think that you have to make extra time to 'carry out' health promotion; rather, you should adopt a way of practice that makes health promotion rooted in the goals and outcomes and the environment of everyday work. For example, there will be a 'culture' in everyday practice in the workplace for infection control, so similarly develop a 'culture' for health promotion practice. The people and patients that you meet in your day-to-day practice will have expectations of the care and support with their problem of the moment. They should also be able to expect that you will take that help forward to support their future wellbeing with health-promoting practice. To be an effective health-promoting nurse involves, as indeed do all areas of practice, updating personal learning and being aware of why and how we go about this.

Continuing with professional development

Continuing to keep skills updated, to learn and extend knowledge for practice, are expected activities for nurses throughout their working lives (NMC, 2008). The NMC states that the people in your care must be able to trust you with their health and wellbeing; further, that you provide a high standard of practice and care at all times.

To keep your skills and knowledge up-to-date:

- have the knowledge and skills for safe and effective practice when working without direct supervision;
- recognise and work within the limits of your competence;
- keep your knowledge and skills up to date throughout your working life;
- take part in appropriate learning and practice activities that maintain and develop your competence and performance (NMC, 2008).

Nurses must therefore make time to keep updated with new developments and research within public health and health promotion in order to be well informed about their practice. At university, as a student, goals for learning and practice have been structured and organised for you. In the future as a qualified nurse you will find that you will have the responsibility for your own learning and updating your practice. If you have developed good study habits and regularly set aside time for updating and reading, then you will find it easier to find the time to continue such professional development activity as you become qualified. Continuing professional development has important implications for accountability to the public. Recipients of care have a right to access practitioners who possess up-to-date knowledge, skills and abilities appropriate to their sphere of practice. This book has suggested that nurses need to address the health promotion needs of their patients wherever care is given. Further, as the development and complexity of organisations continues to grow, there is demand for wider ranges of skills from practitioners. Nurses must therefore be prepared to develop and expand their health-promoting skills.

Thinking about health promotion

Effective health promotion and public health update can involve several activities or elements of personal learning. This may involve being aware of public health at strategic level (see Chapters 3 and 6). It can also be at a more immediate level in day-to-day encounters with your patients (see Chapters 2 and 5). Whatever the level, being aware of recent developments is essential for ensuring that the best possible practices for health promotion are used (NMC, 2008). The Department of Health and organisations such as the NHS, the National Institute for Health and Clinical Excellence (NICE) are sources of public-health-related news, as are organisations such as the British Heart Foundation and Diabetes UK. It is always a good idea to check the websites for recent news and updates, remembering to put in the details of the health topic for the immediate guidelines or update available. For example, checking the NHS guidance for seasonal flu on **www.nhs.uk/conditions/Flu/Pages/Introduction.aspx** or checking the up-to-date guidance on national campaigns such as skin health and sun exposure with the British Association of Dermatologists on **www.bad.org.uk/site/715default.aspx**.

Activity 8.1   *Reflection*

- How confident are you that you have the ability to develop health-promoting practice skills?

Look back on previous practice experience and see areas where health-promoting practice could have been a feature of your encounter with patients.

continued opposite...

continued...

- What, action, if any, have you planned to improve these skills for health promotion practice?
- Could you now explain what health promotion is, having read Chapter 1?
- Do you now understand how it fits into public health, Chapter 6?

As this activity is based on your own skills development, there is no outline answer suggested at the end of the chapter.

Ways of keeping up to date

It makes sense for nurses to develop an understanding of where and how local practice comes about from strategic guidelines and planning. Sometimes you might find yourself having to explain this concept to patients who may think that what is practised locally has been dreamed up by your colleagues, rather than the fact that public health is set to a standard nationally!

One way of keeping up to date is to read the newspapers. The quality broadsheets give more detailed and evidenced-based, in-depth health reports. You may find that the tabloid newspapers only present the views of the reporters and give no references. The in-depth reports that reflect new research, or government health decisions and position statements, can provide topics for you to follow up in your personal updating and continuing development. Often such newspaper reports will give a source for the information, such as a government department or, if it was research, where the original study took place and who has carried it out. In these cases the department can be checked out for further details, or you can carry out a search for the original journal article in which the research was published. Keeping abreast of newspaper health articles is a simple but effective way of maintaining an update. You can be sure that your patients will read the papers and follow health reports. Often they will save up this information to ask you what you think about the subject! Being able to hold a meaningful conversation with patients, which is evidenced-based about current developments, perhaps even correcting a misconception or misunderstanding, is important in establishing a confident and competent manner in day-to-day professional practice.

Activity 8.2   *Reflection*

Think about a past clinical placement and an occasion when you observed or participated in health promotion practice.

- Can you think about how you judged the interaction? What was good about it? What could be improved?
- When you start your next new clinical placement, how do you think you could go about preparing for health-promoting practice?
- How will you update your skills and knowledge for health promotion?

As this activity is based on your own skills development, there is no outline answer suggested at the end of the chapter.

All students find that finance can be an issue! Sharing the expense of subscribing to a relevant professional journal can be a way around this. You may have one or two friends, perhaps more, studying on your course, with whom you could get together. This will lead to you all reading and sharing information and topics for health promotion more immediately. Some students choose to form a study group while at university. This can be a gathering together to discuss coursework for example, but it could also be to discuss aspects of health-promoting practice and share your experiences with each other. Planning time for reading each week is a good habit to develop as a student and if it becomes a regular event on your schedule, it is likely that you will continue with this style of update in the future as a qualified nurse. Setting aside time for reading may be more of a problem for some students than others, however, but there are ways around this. Firstly, have a plan, and then it's more likely to happen. Gather your material together for reading in the first instance, and sort it into priority order to read. Perhaps you have a commitment to reading for a particular total time each week, let's say one hour; you may choose more time. Break this total time into smaller portions of time. This way you can build it into your schedule. Use your travelling time, for example – you could read on the bus or train. Use your break time to read on placement – get yourself a cup of tea or coffee and settle down to update for 20–30 minutes. Use your time while waiting for appointments or waiting to collect children from school. At university, use your time wisely to access computer time in the library for reading on one particular day of the week. Think of all the small portions of time that you could have used to read and update your knowledge of health promotion, and then you have found a way to keep your practice updated.

To summarise:

- read the quality broadsheet newspapers for health articles;
- share the expense with friends with subscription to a relevant professional health journal for sharing reading about health promotion;
- study groups – share with others on your course about health-promoting practice;
- make a plan for reading. Plan for time to read each week. Build your schedule, for example: train or bus journeys, waiting for appointments, waiting to collect children, tea break at work. We suggest a total of 60 minutes each week broken up into two or three manageable portions of time.

The following case study gives an overview of a student's response to preparation for a future clinical placement. She will have to make a plan to keep updated and explore further skills in health promotion practice.

Case study: Preparing for a clinical placement

*Eva has just found out that her next placement will be on the coronary care unit. She has already had a medical ward placement where patients had a mixture of respiratory and cardiac problems. Following a tutorial meeting with her personal development tutor, they discussed what prior knowledge and skills Eva can take with her to this placement. Her personal development tutor has advised that she update herself and prepare for this placement with some background reading. In addition to updating her understanding about the anatomy and physiology of the heart, her tutor suggests that she consults the British Heart Foundation (BHF) website, where she will find out about heart health on **www.bhf.org.uk/**.*

continued opposite...

continued...

Eva revisits her CPR (cardio-pulmonary resuscitation) skills notebook, for the study of emergency life support skills, and reminds herself about the signs and symptoms of myocardial infarction. She is interested to find out from the BHF website that in the UK heart disease kills one in three women as well as one in three men. In fact she discovers that women are three times more likely to die from heart disease than breast cancer, something she had no awareness of. Eva resolves to update herself as much as possible before her placement. She makes a plan to consult the links to 'protecting yourself against heart disease', 'lifestyle advice' and 'risk factors' on the BHF website. She also plans to find out the likely health promotion advice patients will be given in preparation for their discharge from hospital, and what kinds of health promotion support they will need afterwards.

Keeping a record of health promotion practice

A portfolio is a means of keeping a record of development to analyse and evaluate learning and practice. You will probably have had to compile a portfolio of your undergraduate learning and developments while you are studying at university, reflecting your progress on your nursing programme. Your portfolio will be kept for a number of reasons:

- to record professional development and experience;
- to record your reflection on practice;
- to record a focus on work practices;
- to assist you with organising your learning by recording your future aims and targets.

The information stored within your portfolio should be more than a 'what I have done' list of activities. The contents of the portfolio must have a focus on what you have learned, how you can apply this to practice in the future or have applied this to your practice currently. Sometimes students can get lost in their lengthy writing, describing what has happened. They then forget to write or give a very scanty account of what they have learned as a result of the encounter or practice! The balance must be found in explaining what took place, what has been learned and how this may affect future practice and which, if any, changes may take place as a result of this event. Becoming a health-promoting nurse, creating a culture of health promotion in your practice, is a worthy entry in your portfolio, so record your reflection on your health-promoting practice.

The following case study considers a student's reflection following a new experience with health-promoting practice at a health education event.

Case study: Health-promoting practice

Justin is studying for a top-up degree in nursing. As part of his programme of study he has been able to access a health promotion module at degree level. He finds it very relevant to his current post, which is in practice at a genito-urinary medicine outpatients department (GUM clinic). Part of the formative

continued overleaf...

continued...

assessment strategy for the module involves the students working in a team to conduct a health education event, on university premises, in the student union. The event is a health fair led by students (studying on the model with Justin) for students (other undergraduates). This is peer-led health promotion practice. The subject is sexual health education, raising awareness about chlamydia infection. Justin feels that he is up to date with his knowledge about the problems of chlamydia infection, but he finds himself sharing information with the other students in his team and suggests they visit the National Chlamydia Screening Programme website on **www.chlamydiascreening.nhs.uk/ps/index.html**.

What Justin lacks experience in is participating in the running of a health fair. It will be his first experience of health promotion practice at such an event; there is a lot to learn! He will have to select and prepare resources for the health fair, set up an information stall, capture attention of fellow students, engage in health conversation and impart information to students. Hopefully, he can encourage screening for chlamydia and get students to take up testing if appropriate.

All of this health-promoting practice can be recorded in his professional portfolio, as he reflects on his learning experiences and sets out his actions for improving his practice.

Future practice

Once you have become a qualified nurse in your area of practice, you will have continued professional guidance for practice from the NMC code (2008). If you find employment in the NHS, then you will also be following the competence framework to support personal development within the NHS. This is the knowledge and skills framework (KSF) (see also Chapter 7), and it has been designed to:

- identify the knowledge and skills that you need to apply in your post;
- help guide your development;
- provide a fair and objective framework on which to base review and development for all staff;
- provide the basis for career progression in the NHS (DH, 2004b).

The KSF is designed to promote quality care and support staff and is linked to their pay and career progression (RCN, 2005). Each NHS job has a KSF outline which will describe the knowledge and skills that a person is required to have when they apply for a job. This means thinking about your health-promoting skills and how they match the KSF requirements.

Once a year, you and your future line manager will review and appraise your performance, and how you apply your knowledge and skills against the KSF outline. From this process you can then develop a personal development plan (PDP) and this can be kept in your professional portfolio. Some of these development plans could be about you improving on your health-promoting practice skills. The KSF and the development review process are about **lifelong learning**, something that is discussed in a Department of Health policy. *A High Quality workforce: NHS next stage review* (DH, 2008a) gives a strong emphasis on linking clinical practice, academic development and the best use of available evidence for enhancing practice. It further acknowledges the fact that the end of any pre-registration nursing programme is not the end of learning, but is the start of lifelong learning. The KSF will therefore be a critical tool for newly qualified nurses in supporting early career development needs, and portfolios will be an essential way of presenting the evidence of your practice and reflection, providing a focus for discussion at the time of the performance review.

Finally the NMC (2010) explains about the requirement of practice for registered nurses, the professional development, education and training of registrants and their fitness for practice. The standards for post-registration education and practice (PREP) were first introduced in 1995 and registered nurses are required to:

- undertake at least 35 hours of learning activity relevant to practice during the three-year period prior to registration renewal;
- maintain a personal professional portfolio of learning activity;
- comply with any requests from the NMC to audit how these requirements have been met.

All of these structures and guidelines are there to support you in your future practice as a nurse and this will include your health-promoting practice. Your professional portfolio will be different from other students because it is about *you*. It should provide evidence of how you have developed personally and professionally. It should give an account of your achievements and these should include health-promoting practice and any personal development plans for your future learning. In the above case studies, both Justin and Eva had to reflect on what they already knew, what they are learning through current health-promoting practice and what they need to learn in the future. Finally, they would be able to make development plans for their health-promoting role as nurses.

Chapter summary

This chapter has considered the guidance from the NMC (2008) for continuing with your personal and professional development and keeping your skills updated. It has also explored and suggested some ways of keeping updated for health-promoting practice. By reflecting on health promotion practice carried out, nurses are enabled to make sense from the experiences they encounter. Finally it has looked at how you can record this activity in your professional portfolio, by exploring and recording new learning, what you plan to do with it and setting out action plans for further development.

Further reading

Howatson-Jones, L (2010) *Reflective Practice in Nursing.* Exeter: Learning Matters.
A useful text for student nurses introducing reflection; it gives practical help on using reflection techniques.

Hutchfield, K (2010) *Information Skills for Nursing Students.* Exeter: Learning Matters.
A useful text introducing nursing students to key skills in IT, enabling continuation of academic study and professional development.

Useful website

www.nmc-uk.org/

The Nursing and Midwifery Council website. Use the search box on the NMC home page to access your topic.

Glossary

Advocate: Someone who pleads on behalf of another person or group; in health promotion it involves representing the combined efforts of individuals and groups to gain political and social support for a specific health programme or goal.

Continuing professional development: The obligation of professionals to keep themselves up-to-date and competent in theory and practice. Often provided as compulsory or voluntary programmes of study by employers, professional bodies and universities.

Critical consciousness: A widely used concept which was developed by Brazilian educator Paulo Freire. It means that one develops an objective awareness of social, political and economic oppression and takes action against the process of oppression.

Demography: The study of the statistics about population characteristics, i.e. age, gender, social class, ethnicity, race.

Epidemiology: The study of the distribution, determinants and control of disease in populations.

Equity: Fairness – the distribution of resources for health on the basis of need.

External locus of control: A belief that a range of events in your life are occurring regardless of your own effort.

Health agenda: Health issues in the media, public or policy domain ranked according to the amount of time, attention and importance that they are given in discussion, debate and action.

Health behaviour: Activities undertaken by an individual, regardless of actual or perceived health status, for the purpose of promoting, protecting or maintaining health, whether or not such behaviour is objectively effective towards that end (WHO,1998b).

Health gain: A measurable improvement in health status, in individual or a population, attributable to an earlier health intervention.

Health improvement: The area of public health related to improving the health of the population, for instance by tackling obesity, sexually transmitted infections, alcohol and substance misuse and smoking. Sometimes used as a title for organisational functions or planning documents instead of health promotion.

Holistic: An approach that addresses all of the dimensions of health and the whole of someone's life.

Inequalities in health: The gap between the health of different population groups – people from different social classes, ethnic backgrounds or the better and worse off in our society.

Internal locus of control: Belief that the course of your life is largely up to you.

Lay: A term meaning non-professional. It is generally used for patients or community, so the lay viewpoint is that of the patient rather than the nurse or other health professional.

Life skills: Abilities to adopt a positive behaviour that enables individuals to deal effectively with the demands and challenges of everyday life.

Lifelong learning: Learning activity undertaken throughout life either formally or informally.

Lifestyle: The sum total of behaviours that make up the way people live, including leisure and work.

Lobbying: Direct attempts to influence legislation through direct interaction with politicians – petitions, contacting members of parliament, attending public meetings or demonstrating.

NHS local community health services: In England this currently means primary care trusts (PCTs), local organisations responsible for managing health services in the community. There are 152 PCTs which comprised all the community health services and also have the remit for health improvement. They cover the same areas as the local authorities. The current coalition government proposes to transfer health services functions to GP consortia and health improvement to local authorities. The Bill to make these changes is controversial and not yet passed through parliament.

In Northern Ireland Health and Personal Social Services are provided as one integrated service in 19 Health and Social Services (HSS) Trusts.

In Wales, there are 22 local health boards which cover the same areas as the 22 local authorities in Wales. They broadly fulfil the role of the English PCTs.

In Scotland, the NHS is divided into NHS Boards. The role of these Health Boards is the protection and improvement of the health of their respective residents through implementation of The Health Improvement Programme. 63 PCTs operate within the geographical boundaries of individual health boards.

Partnership: Local collaboration by statutory, voluntary and private sector organisations, communities and individuals in planning, implementing and evaluating health promotion.

Peer education: Community programmes in which members of a community or group of people are recruited, trained and supported to carry out health promotion among their peers.

Policy: A broad statement of principles of how to proceed in relation to a specific issue, i.e. national policy on immigration or housing.

Sector: Organisations are usually classified into three types: public sector financed by taxation (NHS and local authorities), private sector (business and commerce) and voluntary sector (charities, not-for-profit and voluntary organisations).

Self-efficacy: Belief in one's capabilities to organise and execute the actions required to manage prospective situations.

Self-esteem: The extent to which a person regards himself or herself to be of value. Essential for feeling good about yourself and taking action for yourself.

Social class: A measure of a person's position in society.

Social exclusion: The inability of certain groups or individuals to participate fully in life due to structural inequalities in access to social, economic, political and cultural resources.

Social inclusion: Activities designed to address and reverse social exclusion.

Socio-economic status: A way of classifying social class by income levels, or occupations, which have an effect on lifestyle.

Strategy: A broad plan of actions that specifies what is to be achieved, how and when. It provides a framework for planning.

Victim blaming: An approach to health education which emphasises individual action and does not address external forces that influence the individual person. In other words, blaming the victim of an illness for not acting to improve their health.

References

Acheson, D (1988) *Public Health in England*. London: HMSO.

Atkin, WS, Edwards, R, Kralj-Hans, I, Wooldrage, K, Hart, A, Northover, JMA, Parkin, DM, Wardle, J, Duffy, SW and Cuzick, J (2010) Once only flexible sigmoidoscopy screening in prevention of colorectal cancer: a multicentre randomised controlled trial. *Lancet*, 375 (9726): 1624–33.

Ajzen, I and Fishbein, M (1980) *Understanding Attitudes and Predicting Social Behaviour.* Englewood Cliffs, NJ: Prentice Hall.

Babor, TF and Higgins-Biddle, JC (2001) *Brief Intervention for Hazardous and Harmful Drinking: a manual for use in primary care*. Geneva: World Health Organization.

Bandura, A (1977) Self-Efficacy: Toward a Unifying Theory of Behaviour Change. *Psychological Review*, 84: 191–215.

Becker, MH (ed.) (1974) *The Health Belief Model and Personal Health Behaviour.* New Jersey: Slack.

Bloom, BS (1984) *Taxonomy of Educational Objectives. Handbook 1: Cognitive Domain*. London: Longman.

Bowen, RL, Duffy, SW, Ryan, DA, Hart, IR and Jones, JL (2008) Early onset of breast cancer in a group of British black women, *British Journal of Cancer*, 98: 227–81.

Bradshaw, JR (1972) The concept of social need. *New Society*, 496: 640–43.

British Heart Foundation (2009) *Blood Pressure; Beating Heart Disease Together*. London: BHF.

Burford, D, Kirby, M and Austoker, J (2010) *Prostate Cancer Risk Management Programme Information for Primary Care; PSA testing in asymptomatic men. Evidence Document.* NHS Cancer Screening Programmes **www.cancerscreening.co.uk**.

Cabe, J, Kirk, S, Nelson, P, Greenwood, D and Bojke, L (2006) *Can Peer Education Influence People with Diabetes? Final Report to the FSA*. Available on **www.foodbase.org.uk/admintools/report documents/91-1-449_91_146_EPP_final_report_04-09-06_as_sent.pdf**

Cancer Research UK (2008) *Increasing uptake of NHS cancer screening services: a Screening Matters report*. London: Cancer Research UK.

Cancer Research UK (2009) *Breast Cancer in Men*. London: Cancer Research UK.

Cancer Research UK (2010) *Science update blog*. London: Cancer Research UK. Available on **http://scienceblog.cancerresearchuk.org/2010/04/28/new-study-marks-major-advance-in-bowel-cancer**.

Department of Health (1992) *The Health of the Nation: A Strategy for Health in England*. London: HMSO.

Department of Health (1998) *Saving Lives: Our Healthier Nation*. London: HMSO.

Department of Health (2001a) *National Service Framework for Diabetes: Standards*. London: Department of Health.

Department of Health (2001b) *The Expert Patient – a new approach to chronic disease management for the 21st Century*. London: The Stationery Office.

Department of Health (2003a) *National Service Framework for Diabetes: Delivery of standards*. London: Department of Health.

Department of Health (2003b) *Toolkit for Producing Patient Information*. London: Department of Health. Available from **www.dh.gov.uk/en/Publicationsandstatistics/Publications/PublicationsPolicyAndGuidance/DH_4070141**.

Department of Health (2004a) *Choosing Health: making healthy choices easier.* London: HMSO.

Department of Health (2004b) *The NHS Knowledge and Skills Framework and the Development Review Process.* London: Department of Health.

Department of Health (2005) *National Service Framework for Long Term Conditions.* London: HMSO.

Department of Health (2006a) *Our Health Our Care Our Say.* London: Department of Health.

Department of Health (2006b) *Be Breast Aware.* London: Department of Health. Available on **www.dh. gov.uk/en/Publicationsandstatistics/Publications/PublicationsPolicyAndGuidance/DH_062697**.

Department of Health (2007) *Health Literacy.* London: Department of Health.

Department of Health (2008a) *A High Quality Workforce: NHS next stage review.* London: Department of Health.

Department of Health (2008b) *High Quality Care for All: The next stage review final report.* London: Department of Health.

Department of Health (2009a) *NHS Health Check: vascular risk assessment and management best practice guidance.* London: Department of Health. Available on **www.dh.gov.uk/en/Publicationsandstatistics/Publications/PublicationsPolicyAndGuidance/DH_097489**.

Department of Health (2009b) *Your Health Your Way: A guide to long term conditions and self care.* London: Department of Health.

Department of Health (2010a) *Healthy Lives, Healthy People: our strategy for public health in England.* London: Department of Health.

Department of Health (2010b) *Improving the Health and Wellbeing of People with Long Term Conditions.* London: Department of Health.

Department of Health (2010c) *Screening: Health Care.* London: Department of Health. Available on **www. dh.gov.uk/en/Healthcare/Cancer/Screening/DH_106687**.

Gok, M, Heideman, D, van Kemenade, F, Berkhof, J, Rozendaal L, Spruyt J, Voorhurst F, Belien J, Babovic M, Snijders P and Meijer C (2010) HPV testing on self collected cervicovaginal lavage specimens as screening method for women who do not attend cervical screening: cohort study. *British Medical Journal*, online, 340: 1040.

Hardyman, R, Hardy, P, Brodie, J and Stephens, R (2005) It's good to talk: comparison of a telephone helpline and website for cancer information. *Patient Education and Counseling*, 57 (3) 315–20.

Iddo, G and Prigat, A (2004) Why organisations continue to create patient information leaflets with readability and usability problems: an exploratory study. *Health Education Research*, 20 (4): 485–93.

Joint Health Surveys Unit (2008) *Health Survey for England 2006: CVD and Risk Factors Adults, Obesity and Risk Factors Children.* London: TSO.

Kopans, D (2010) Screening for Breast Cancer among women in their 40s. *The Lancet Oncology*, 11 (12): 1108–9.

Lorig, K, Mazonson, P and Holman, HR (1993) Evidence suggesting that health education for self-management in patients with chronic arthritis has sustained health benefits while reducing health care costs. *Arthritis and Rheumatism*, 36 (4): 439–46.

MARBIS study group (2005) Screening with magnetic resonance imaging and mammography of a UK population at high familial risk of breast cancer: a prospective multicentre cohort study. *The Lancet*, 365 (9473): 1769–78.

Marmot, M (2010) *Fair Society, Healthy Lives: Strategic Review of Health Inequalities in England.* London: The Marmot Review. Available at **www.marmotreview.org/**.

Mencap Accessibility Team (2008) *Make it Clear: a guide to easy read information.* London: Mencap.

National Health Service (2010) *Patient Information.* Available on **www.nhsidentity.nhs.uk/tools-and-resources/patient-information.**

National Health Service (2011) *NHS Abdominal Aortic Aneurysm screening programme.* Available on **http://aaa.screening.nhs.uk/**.

National Institute for Health and Clinical Excellence (2007) *Behaviour Change at Population, Community and Individual Levels. Public Health Guidance 6.* London: NICE.

National Screening Committee UK (2010) *Screening programmes.* UK National Screening Committee Screening Portal website: **http://webarchive.nationalarchives.gov.uk/20100407120701/screening.nhs.uk/**.

Nightingale, F (1859) *Notes on Nursing: What it is and What it is Not.* Virginia: Wilder Publications (2007).

Nursing and Midwifery Council (2008) *The Code: Standards of conduct, performance and ethics for nurses and midwives.* London: NMC.

Nursing and Midwifery Council (2010) *The PREP Handbook.* London: NMC.

Office for National Statistics (2010) Internet Access. **www.statistics.gov.uk/cci/nugget.asp?id=8.**

Office of the Public Guardian (2009) *Making Decisions: A guide for family, friends and other unpaid carers, the Mental Capacity Act* (4th edn). London: Crown Copyright.

Prochaska, JO and DiClemente, CC (1982) Transtheoretical therapy: Toward a more integrative model of change. *Psychotherapy: Theory Research and Practice*, 20: 161–73.

Rollnick, S, Miller, WR and Butler, CC (2008) *Motivational Interviewing in Health Care: helping patients change behaviour.* New York: Guilford Press.

Rotter, JB (1966) Generalised Expectancies for Internal and External Control of Reinforcement. *Psychological Monographs* 80 (609): 1–28.

Royal College of Nursing (2005) *NHS Knowledge and Skills Framework: outlines for nursing posts. RCN guidance for nurses and managers in creating KSF outlines in the NHS.* London: RCN.

Royal National Institute of Blind People (2004) *See it right pack.* London: RNIB.

Rozendaal L, Spruyt, J, Voorhorst, F, Belien, J, Babovic, M, Snijders, P and Meijer, C (2010) HPV testing on self collected cervico-vaginal lavage specimens as screening method for women who do not attend cervical screening: cohort study. *British Medical Journal*, 340: 1040.

Skills for Health (2004) *Public Health National Occupational Standards – practice and specialists.* Bristol: Skills for Health.

Tannahill, A (1985) What is health promotion?, *Health Education Journal*, **44**: 167–68.

Tannahill, A (2009) The Tannahill Model Revisited. *Public Health*, 123 (5): 396–99.

Tones, BK and Tilford, S (2001) *Health Promotion; Effectiveness, efficiency and Equity*, 3rd edn. Cheltenham: Stanley Thornes.

Wallis, L (2010) Back behind the Counter, *Nursing Standard*, 25 (2): 62–63.

Wanless, D (2002) *Securing Our Future Health: Taking A Long-Term View – an independent review.* London: HM Treasury.

Weller, DP and Campbell, C (2009) Uptake in cancer screening programmes: a priority in cancer control, *British Journal of Cancer*, 101 (S2): S55–S59.

Williams, M, Poulter, MR, Davis, M, McInnes, GT, Potter, JF, Sever, PS and Thom, SM (2004) Guidelines for management of hypertension: report of the fourth working party of the British Hypertension Society, 2004 – BHS IV. *Journal of Human Hypertension*, 18, 139–85.

World Health Assembly (1998) *Health for all policy for the twenty-first century. (Resolution WHA51.7)*. Geneva: WHO, **http://dataplan.info/cb21/archiv/material/worldhealthdeclaration.pdf**.

World Health Organization (1948) *Constitution of the World Health Organization*. Geneva: WHO, **www.who.int/governance/eb/who_constitution_en.pdf**.

World Health Organization (1978) *Primary Health Care: The Alma Ata Conference*. Geneva: WHO, **www.who.int/hpr/NPH/docs/declaration_almaata.pdf**.

World Health Organization (1986) *The Ottawa Charter: first international conference on health promotion*. Geneva: WHO, **www.who.int/hpr/NPH/docs/ottawa_charter_hp.pdf**.

World Health Organization (1988) *Adelaide Recommendations on Healthy Public Policy*. Geneva: WHO, **www.who.int/healthpromotion/conferences/previous/adelaide/en/index.html**.

World Health Organization (1991) *Third International Conference on Health Promotion (Sundsvall)*. Geneva: WHO, **www.who.int/healthpromotion/conferences/previous/sundsvall/en/**.

World Health Organization (1997) *Jakarta Declaration on Health Promotion into the 21st Century*. Geneva: WHO, **www.who.int/healthpromotion/conferences/previous/jakarta/declaration/en/**.

World Health Organization (1998a) *Health 21: health for All in the 21st century*. Geneva: WHO, **www.euro.who.int/__data/assets/pdf_file/0003/88590/EHFA5-E.pdf**.

World Health Organization (1998b) *Health Promotion Glossary*. Geneva: WHO, **www.who.int/hpr/NPH/docs/hp_glossary_en.pdf**.

World Health Organization (2005) *Bangkok Charter for Health Promotion in a Globalised World*. Geneva: WHO, **www.who.int/healthpromotion/conferences/6gchp/en/index.html**.

World Health Organization (2009) *7th Global Conference on Health Promotion: track themes. Track 2 Health literacy and health behavior*. Geneva: WHO, **www.who.int/healthpromotion/conferences/7gchp/track2/en/index.html**.

Index

Note: Page number in italics refers to figures, illustrations, and tables.

teaching, patients
  approaches for conducting 59
  barriers to learning 59–60
  Bloom's taxonomy (or levels) of learning *60*
  electronic media for 65–6
  evaluation of 66–7
  group teaching 63–4
  and health literacy 67–8
  levels of learning 60–1
  as part of nursing care 67
  planning for 61–3
  poor teaching environment, case study 58
  skills required for 63
  teaching session
    place for 59
    planning for 62
  written information as aid for 64–5
Terrence Higgins Trust 28
thalassemia 44

Tones' empowerment model, for promotion of self-management 84
tubal infertility 53

U
UK National Screening Committee 44, 45, 48
UK national strategic policies, for public health and health promotion 16–17

V
vascular risk, health check programme for 51
victim blaming 18, 19

W
Weight Wins scheme 36
wellness model, of health 10–11, 13
WINDFAL programme 81

X
X-PERT structured education programme 81